The Factory House at Oporto

Early model of the Factory House

The Factory House
at Oporto

JOHN DELAFORCE

CHRISTOPHER HELM PUBLISHERS LTD
in association with
CHRISTIE'S WINE PUBLICATIONS
Bicentenary Edition 1990

© 1990 John Delaforce

First published 1979 by Christie's Wine Publications
Second, revised edition published in 1983 by Christie's Wine Publications
Third, revised and expanded bicentenary edition 1990 published by
Christopher Helm (Publishers) Ltd,
Imperial House, 21–25 North Street, Bromley,
Kent BR1 1SB
in association with Christie's Wine Publications

ISBN 0-7470-0614-8

A CIP catalogue record for this book is available from the British Library.

Typeset in Singapore by: Letraprint
Printing and bound in Singapore by: Stamford Press (Pte) Ltd

To Valerie
whose constant encouragement
enabled me to persevere
with the writing of this book

Contents

Illustrations

Acknowledgements

The frontispiece and the illustrations on pages 9, 51, 73 and 91 are reproduced by courtesy of the Conway Library, Courtauld Institute of Art, London.

The documents on pages 18 and 19 are Crown Copyright and are reproduced by kind permission of the Public Record Office, London.

The illustration on page 24 is reproduced by courtesy of Sandeman & Co. The illustrations on pages 30, 49 and 79 are reproduced by permission of the Council of the British Church of St James, Oporto, Warre & Co., and Cockburn Smithes & Co., respectively.

The painting on the front cover is reproduced by kind permission of the Clube Portuense, Oporto.

Foreword

This is the story of a building. It stands at the corner of two busy streets in the City of Oporto, not far from the River Douro.

Two centuries ago these streets were in the centre of the commercial and residential area of the city; now their importance has diminished and their situation become unfashionable, but the Factory House continues to be a reminder of the British presence in the Port Wine trade, unbroken for more than three centuries, as well as an elegant memorial to the merchants and factors of an age when the British influence upon the architecture and artistic and social life in Oporto was considerable, marking the beginning of the special relationship that still exists between the British and the Portuguese in the North of Portugal.

The story is set against the background of the 'Factories' in the 17th and 18th centuries and of the formation of the Association of British Port shippers in the early 19th century, with the Factory House forming the central theme, and this work describes the early history and customs, as well as the contents, of this remarkable and possibly unique building.

This revised third edition is being published to coincide with the bicentenary of the Factory House in 1990 and contains additional material to the previous editions of 1979 and 1983. In spite of the lack of records from the years prior to the Peninsular War, it should provide as complete a record as possible about a subject of much historical and social interest.

My acknowledgements to Croft & Co. and Offley Forrester & Co. for allowing me to examine their archives and to A.A. Ferreira and Taylor Fladgate & Yeatman for permission to consult the records of Hunt Roope & Co. and the Joseph Camo letters respectively. Also I am grateful to the Members of the Factory House and to their firms for the encouragement and support I have received from them.

I am indebted to Christie's Wine Publications for publishing the first two editions of this work and for sponsoring this edition in association with the Publishers, and to Rosemary Ward in particular for all her help.

Finally, my thanks to the Editor, Carolyn Burch, for correcting the proofs and for incorporating much additional material with the text of the previous edition.

John Delaforce,
Oporto, 1989

1

Definitions of Factory and Factory Houses ☆ History of early Factories in India, Africa and Europe

Any research into the history and origins of the British Factory in the north of Portugal and in particular at Oporto, is greatly handicapped by the scarcity of documents and records available on the subject. Similarly, few details have survived about the Factory House prior to 1811.

It is a coincidence that in the case of both the Lisbon and Oporto Factories many records were said to have been taken to England by the respective Consuls when the French invaded Portugal in 1807 and were subsequently not traced. However, as will be described later, there exists considerable doubt as to exactly which records really went to England, and whether in fact many never left Portugal but were subsequently lost or destroyed.

It is essential to emphasise the difference in meaning, not always appreciated by many writers, between the British Factory and the Factory House. The former was the name used to describe the British merchants or factors collectively, in the sense of a business guild or association, and the latter is the name given to the actual building used by them as their headquarters. In Oporto the British Factory only used the present House under that title during the years 1790–1807 because most of the members left the country in 1807 until 1810 or 1811 and by then the Factory had been abolished. Since 1814 the House has been the headquarters of the British Association, composed of British port wine shippers, with their partners and directors as the individual members. At the present time there are 12 member firms. The basic membership of the Association and ownership of the House has always rested with the firms and this was confirmed in 1802 at the time of the death of John Whitehead, when various Resolutions were recorded in the names of the Treasurer and of 14 member firms.

It is likely that the term 'Factory House' was not used in Oporto prior to the building of the present House in 1786–90, although various small houses were owned or rented earlier by the Consul or the members and used by the Factory. Similarly the name British Factory gradually disappeared after the Treaty of 1810 and the formation of the British Association on the 21st November 1814, although it is true that in a different context there are frequent references in the first half of the 19th century by James Forrester and others to the *Feitoria* and 'Feitoria Wines' and these will be referred to in more detail in a later chapter.

The origin of the term 'Factory' and the Portuguese equivalent, *Feitoria*, needs some explanation.

The dictionary definitions of a Factory make it plain that the original sense of the word was 'an establishment for traders carrying on business in a foreign country' as well as 'the body of factors in any one place'. The origin of the word is from mediaeval Latin *factoria*, subsequently found in several of the

[1]

View of Oporto across the river from Vila Nova de Gaia, dated 1881 by C. Napier Hemy, R.A.

Romantic languages, as the Spanish *factoria*, Italian *fattoria* and of course the Portuguese *feitoria*. There can be little doubt that the English equivalents, 'factory' and 'factor' derived originally from the Portuguese, and A. H. Walford in his *British Factory in Lisbon* published in 1940, is also of the same opinion.

The earliest Portuguese *feitorias* were those established in West Africa during the first voyages of discovery in the 15th century. Like those subsequently in East Africa, India and the Far East, their purpose was to serve as bases, often fortified, for the purchase, barter or seizure and subsequent storage, of the goods that each region produced, until such time as a ship was available to bring them to Lisbon. The first Portuguese *feitoria* was at Arguim, south of Cape Blanco, in what is now Mauritania, established about 1443. This was a century and a half before the British built their first factory in India. Arguim was a fortified castle and there was a considerable trade in gold dust, ivory and slaves which were exchanged for horses, cloth, brassware and corn from Portugal, and these had in many cases first been imported from N. Europe.

The business in gold was very important and subsequent *feitorias* in Senegal and Gambia were used to divert the gold which formerly went across the Sahara from the upper reaches of the Niger and Volta rivers. However, as the

The Factory House at Oporto

discoverers gradually sailed southwards, new *feitorias* superseded the earlier ones in importance and the greatest of these was the castle at S. Jorge da Mina, on the Gold Coast, built in the late 15th century. The Portuguese rarely established *feitorias* inland and their jurisdiction seldom extended beyond the coastal areas.

After Bartholomeu Dias rounded the Cape of Good Hope in 1488 the way was open for further trading posts in East Africa and along the route to India and the East, to capture the spice trade. Two important *feitorias* were at Sofala, established in 1505, and at Moçambique island two years later. The former continued for over a century and an English writer referred to it in 1613 as 'where the Portugals have a Fort and Factorie of very rich trade'.

In India, Goa was captured in 1510 and supplanted in importance the earlier *feitorias* at Calicut and Cochin which had been established about 1500 during the voyage of Pedro Alvares Cabral. Control of the Persian Gulf was secured by the seizure of Ormuz in 1515. The principal trade was in spices, which consisted of cloves from the Moluccas, cinnamon from Ceylon, and pepper, mace, nutmeg and ginger, many of which were shipped from the *feitoria* at Malacca in Malaysia. On arrival at Lisbon the spices were sent for distribution in northern Europe, to the Crown *feitorias* at Antwerp and Bruges, the latter according to one source dating from 1386. The Antwerp trading centre, known as the *Feitoria de Flandres*, was discontinued in 1549, as it was unable to compete favourably with the local traders.

The situation changed rapidly in the early 17th century, with the Dutch colonial expansion in the Far East and the establishment of the Factories of the Dutch East India Company with their headquarters at Batavia from 1619. Many of the Portuguese settlements, such as those in Ceylon and the Malabar Coast, were captured by the Dutch, who later extended their influence as far as West Africa and ousted the Portuguese from the Gold Coast. All that was to remain of the Portuguese empire in the Far East were Macao, Timor and Goa.

In the British context, the Portuguese had anticipated them in India by about a hundred years. The East India Company, granted their charter by Elizabeth I in 1600, built the first British Factory at Surat, north of Bombay, in 1613. By 1647 they had no less than 23 in India. They served several purposes, being trading posts and warehouses for storing the goods such as spices and indigo before shipment to England, as well as providing residences and offices for their factors and for the company officials who acted as political administrators over large areas of the Indian sub-continent.

In 1638, the factors at Surat were described as 'leading a collegiate life'. The Factory was managed by a President and a Council, with their own preacher and surgeon, protected by a guard of English soldiers. They evidently lived in great style and 'at meals trumpets ushered in the courses'. This custom was prevalent in the large country houses in England where, from mediaeval times until early in the 18th century, it was usual for the meals to be accompanied by music and for a fanfare of trumpets to herald the entrance of a procession bringing in each course.

It was also recorded that 'the English in 1640 built a wall and within it a college for the Factors and Merchants at Madras' which they called Fort St. George.

The Portuguese *feitorias* in India were not established or maintained by private trading companies but were Crown monopolies managed by the

[3]

officers of the King and defended by troops. Their prime purpose was to collect the products, mainly spices, acquired in India and the Far East for shipment to Portugal, but they also had a considerable religious significance as the missionary priests who accompanied the discoverers aimed to further the spread of Christianity, namely the Roman Catholic faith. It was said by Vasco da Gama's men that they had gone in search of Christians and spices, but in fact it was only later in the second half of the 16th century that really stern measures were taken by the Jesuits against the Muslims and Hindus in an attempt to secure conversions. While not actually trying to convert by force, destroying the mosques and temples made the practice of their religion very difficult. Less repressive measures had to be taken at Ormuz on the Persian Gulf where the population was almost entirely Muslim and the Portuguese were anxious not to antagonise the neighbouring Persians.

The restrictions imposed by the Jesuits in the Portuguese empire resembled those against the Protestants in Portugal by the Inquisition and their worship had to be in private. The same complaints were made of Hindu children being forcibly taken and sent to Jesuit colleges as were voiced of Protestant children being kidnapped in Portugal.

But no real comparison can be drawn between the Portuguese Factories in India and those of the East India Company and the Factories of various nationalities in Europe. The former were built by pioneers in a strange and hostile land and were, in addition to being trading posts, also fortresses to protect their merchants from attacks by the local tribes, who in many cases did not hesitate to attempt to drive out the invaders. The same certainly applied in the case of the Portuguese *feitorias* in Africa, where it was essential to build a fort to protect the merchants and the goods stored within their warehouses.

The term *feitoria* or factory has had many different meanings over the years, and whereas in the collective sense it has invariably been used to describe the merchants and factors as a body, yet when applied to the buildings used by them it could mean either a warehouse for storage of goods, a residential headquarters and offices for the large trading companies, often with several smaller factories in the same country, and finally a house for purely social purposes. This seems to have been the case with the Oporto Factory House for which the design was clearly conceived with social entertainments in mind.

It is true that subsequently the entrance hall of the Oporto Factory House was said to have been used by the merchants or factors as a meeting place of business, but even that was doubted by one writer, John Milford Jnr., who wrote of a visit to Oporto in 1812–13 'in the middle of the street fronting my hotel, the Exchange is held, but to my observation the daily meeting of the Merchants appeared more like a rendezvous of loungers to settle the important engagements of the evening than for the transactions of business'. Milford also had the same impression of the merchants when they were inside the Factory House.

W. H. Harrison, in 1839, wrote: 'the ground floor is devoted to the purposes of an exchange, although at present it is less used as a place of mercantile rendezvous than the street in which it stands'.

For a closer or inside view, Arthur Hunt, Treasurer in 1832, wrote to Lord Palmerston, 'the House called the Factory House is, in the strictest sense of the word, a Club House similar to any of the London Club Houses'.

[4]

The Factory House at Oporto

In the middle of the 17th century, there were several foreign Factories in Lisbon, notably German, French, Spanish, Italian and Dutch, and the British had close links with the latter who shared equal rights in the British Burial Ground. Many of these still existed in the 18th century. In *A Picture of Lisbon* 1809, by 'A Gentleman many years resident in Lisbon', mention is made of a French Factory Church dedicated to St. Louis, and an Italian Church to Our Lady of Loretto.

The British Factories in Europe were in some cases established even earlier than those in India and they were often linked to trading companies, such as the Hamburg Company with a Factory from the beginning of the 17th century until 1808, when 'a place of Divine Worship was supported out of the funds of the factory'. Also the Russia Company with Factories at St. Petersburg, Cronstadt and Archangel, abolished by the Tsar in 1807. The Levant Company was very important and was empowered to levy duties on British goods imported into the Ottoman Empire. Incorporated in 1581 by Royal Charter, the Company paid the British Consul out of the revenue and even the first British Ambassador to Turkey in 1606. It is significant that when the Consul at Smyrna was asked to draw up a list of the property belonging to the Company he included the Consular House, a Chapel, the Chaplain's residence and the hospital, but there was no mention of any Factory House. This has been confirmed in more recent times, to the effect that no Factory House was known to have ever existed at Smyrna.

Many of the Factories ceased to exist about 1825, including those in Brazil, at Cadiz and Port St. Mary's in Spain and at Leghorn. The last named was established in 1736 and from their Fund a British Protestant Chapel was built and a burial ground purchased. At Gothenburg a British Factory still exists, dating from the second half of the 17th century and with the original title, but apparently they have never had their own House.

Most, if not all, of these Factories were financed by Contribution Funds, on the same lines as those in Oporto which will be described later.

The Consul in Lisbon wrote to the Secretary of State in London in 1720 on the difficulty of collecting the Contribution Fund and also referred to the British Factories in Spain.

In Portugal itself, in addition to those at Lisbon, Oporto and Viana do Castelo, Factories were recorded in 1702 by Paul Methuen, the British Resident in Lisbon, who reported to the Foreign Office that he had written to the Factories at Coimbra and Faro. The mention of Coimbra is remarkable in that Factories in whatever country they were established were invariably in the coastal towns, as their members were engaged in the import and export of merchandise and would normally have their offices in the seaports. It is therefore open to doubt whether an inland town such as Coimbra could in fact have had a Factory of any importance, although its existence is confirmed by a letter dated September 1732 from Lord Tyrawley, the British Ambassador to Lisbon, to the Duke of Newcastle in which he refers 'to the Factories at Oporto and Coimbra'.*

There was a considerable trade to the north of Europe in spices from the East and wine from the Minho district of Portugal, and it is probable that as a result of the wine business the British Factory at Viana do Castelo came into existence at the end of the 16th century or early in the 17th century.

*Public Record Office S.P. 89/37

Chapter 1

2

The British in the North of Portugal ☆ Early wine shipments from Viana do Castelo and the Douro ☆ First references to Oporto Factory ☆ Appointment of Judge Conservator ☆ Factory Chaplains ☆ The Expulsion of Reverend Samuel Barton ☆ The Factory and Merchants of Oporto and their grievances in the 17th century

British merchants had settled in Viana do Castelo, at the mouth of the River Lima, about 45 miles north of Oporto, as well as at Melgaço and Monção on the River Minho, at an earlier date than at Oporto itself. John Croft in his *Treatise on the Wines of Portugal* (1788) believed that they did not settle in Portugal until after the Treaty of 1654 and that before then 'they went only as Super-Cargoes and returned again to England'.

If that is correct, it means that the period in which they were engaged in the shipment of Minho wines was relatively short, because by 1678 if not earlier some wine shippers had turned their attention to the Douro wine region and started to ship from Oporto. In that year the first recorded statistics reveal that 408 pipes were exported.

However some firms continued in the Minho for more than a century, and in 1698 there is a record of John Page living at Viana and in 1703 of Thos. Woodmass tasting wines at Melgaço and Monção, some miles inland on the River Minho. One writer mentioned a house belonging to Mr. Noble at Viana as late as 1845. Hunt Roope Newman had warehouses at Viana do Castelo c.1654 and even earlier they were importing Newfoundland dried codfish (*bacalhau*) which was re-exported from Dartmouth.

Croft had mentioned that 'before the introduction of the Ports, there were also imported the wines of Ribadavia from Galicia a province in Spain'. This district is further inland and higher up the River Minho, and it is possible that Croft was mistaken in his suggestion that some British actually lived there. They could of course have bought wines from there as well as from the Portuguese Minho wine districts.

W. H. Kingston, writing on this subject in 1845: 'I cannot learn the year when Port wine was first introduced into England, though I believe about two or three centuries ago only it was used as a medicine and sold for that purpose in the shops of the apothecaries. It was at that time produced on the romantic banks of the Lima, a river running into the sea at Viana, where the first British merchants settled and whence they shipped it to England.'

The wines themselves, usually described as 'Red Portugal', were certainly of lower alcoholic content than those subsequently shipped from the Douro district, being grown in what is now the region of Vinho Verde, but brandy was added on shipment to enable the wine to stand the voyage and arrive in a drinkable condition. They must have been thin astringent wines, hardly worthy of Seller's description as being similar to burgundy. He was evidently confusing the Minho wines with those shipped later from the Douro district.

It was certainly a demand for fuller-bodied and higher-strength wines that caused the eventual end of the shipment of Minho wines to England. It is interesting that at the present time, about three hundred years later, some white wines (vinho verde) are being shipped to England and attempts are being made to popularise this type in this important market.

However, if the Minho wines in the 17th century were not of the highest class, the casks in which they were shipped, evidently at first made by coopers brought from England, must have been good and Woodmass wrote that 'the English coopers are a drunken lot but ye natives now know how to make casks'.

There was apparently plenty of social life at Viana do Castelo and Woodmass was well entertained there, meeting the Consul and 'Ye Clergyman'. The identity of the latter is unknown, as there is no record of the existence of any Chaplain in Oporto at that date. He was clearly a sporting parson, as we read 'after dinner some Portugal cockerels did engaged in battle. Ye Minister directing'. He was possibly one of the unlicensed clergy in the Diocese, whose method of appointment and behaviour was the subject of much criticism. As recently as the latter part of the 19th century Bishop Sandford considered that 'the prevailing character of Continental Chaplains became a byword and a reproach to the English Church'.

A writer in the *Journal Horticolo-Agricola*, published in 1903, stated that the British Factory transferred to Oporto from Viana do Castelo in the middle of the 17th century. There appears to have been no 'House' there belonging to the Factory; at least there is no mention of any such building in *Portugal Antigo e Moderno* (Pinho Leal, 1882), which gives a detailed description of all the houses of importance in Viana do Castelo at that period.

In documents at the Public Record Office and the British Library there are frequent references, during the second half of the 17th century, to the British Merchants of Oporto, but the first mention of the Factory occurs in 1666 in correspondence from Sir Robert Southwell who was in Lisbon to negotiate a new Treaty of Commerce. He had written to the merchants of Oporto who had been complaining that the Treaty of 1654 had been violated and he specifically referred to the Factory. In fact their complaints continued for some years and in 1675 the British Minister in Lisbon, Francis Parry, wrote to the Secretary of State that the members of the English Factory of Oporto complained of grievances contrary to the Article of Peace. This referred to the Treaty between Cromwell and King D. João IV, for which negotiations had begun in 1653 and which was primarily a commercial alliance.

However, an important objective for the Protestant British merchants was to obtain some safeguards from the Inquisition and these seem to have been promised to a certain extent in 1654 when preliminary rights were granted. The final ratification of the Treaty only came in 1656. But in spite of this, the grievances were to continue for many years, mostly caused by the antagonism of the Inquisition, which among other actions was accused of arresting Jews who owed money to English merchants, whose debts were therefore not paid. The merchants also complained 'that in spite of the friendship that should exist between the nations, they stick not to call us Hereticks and doggs'.

In such an atmosphere, it is hardly surprising that no Chaplain was yet permitted in Oporto, and the first mention of this possibility was a letter from

Southwell to the Factory in Oporto in January 1667.*

One of the privileges granted to the British by the Treaty of 1654 was the appointment of a magistrate or lawyer to act as arbitrator in disputes, mostly in connection with the import duties and tariffs payable on British imports, and to settle claims by the British merchants and to help them with the collection of debts from Portuguese buyers.

The appointment of this official, whose title was Judge Conservator (*Juiz Conservador*) was made at first only in Lisbon and he was appointed to cover the whole country. But in 1691 the Oporto Factory were granted their own Conservator who was paid a retaining fee out of Factory funds and it was a much sought after post.

The nomination of the Conservator by the merchants evidently led to abuses and the British Envoy Lord Tyrawley writing from Lisbon to the Secretary of State Fox in 1755 was critical of the Lisbon merchants whose method of nominating or attempting to choose the Conservator he described as incorrect.

'I have known many inconveniences attending their intermeddling in these elections and all such Factory Officers can only be at the nomination of the King's Minister, otherwise each merchant will vote for such a Judge to be Conservator before whom he has a case depending . . . and the great seizure of money that sent me last to Portugal was absolutely made on a certain merchant from a disobligation a Judge owed him for not giving him vote to be Conservator, though by a mistake they seized the money of another person instead of him on whom they intended this revenge'.

The Lisbon Factory meetings did not please the Envoy. 'This meeting too is an absurdity from the Persons who compose it, for any low fellow that keeps a wine house or a Barber's shop, that once has paid the Contribution settled by Act of Parliament for perhaps a box of Hatts or Stockings has as much title to goe to that meeting and talk as much nonsense as he pleases as if he was the head of the best house in Lisbon'.**

The appointment of Conservator was confirmed in the Treaty of 1810, Article X, as well as the method by which it was made.

'His Royal Highness is pleased to grant them (the subjects of Great Britain within his Dominions) the privilege of nominating and having special Magistrates to act as Judges Conservators. These Judges shall try and decide all causes brought before them by British Subjects in the same manner as formerly. They shall be chosen by the plurality of British Subjects residing in or trading at the Port or Place where the Jurisdiction of the Judge Conservator is to be established and the choice so made shall be transmitted to His Britannic Majesty's Ambassador or Minister resident at the Court of Portugal, to be by him laid before His Royal Highness the Prince Regent of Portugal in order to obtain His Royal Highness' consent and confirmation'.

The appointment of a Judge Conservator, also sometimes described as *Desembargador*, or Chief Judge of Appeal, ceased in Oporto with the final payment of Rs. 300$000 (£75) for the year 1826, subsequent to the abolition of the Contribution Fund which will be described later. The post was still in existence in Lisbon in 1848.

No fixed date can be attributed to the establishment of the Factory in

*British Library, Southwell papers Add. 34336.
**Tyrawley Papers. British Library Add. MS 23634.

The Factory House at Oporto

*'he Revd. Samuel Barton,
reacher to the Factory at
)porto, 1682–3*

Oporto and it must certainly have evolved gradually. One of the earliest references can be found in documents referring to the appointment of the first British Chaplain, John Brawlerd, who was sent to Oporto by the Bishop of London in 1671. He was described as 'preaching to the Factory on the Lord's Day and on certain holydays'. The circumstances of his appointment and departure from Oporto in 1675 are related in the author's *Anglicans Abroad* (S.P.C.K., London 1982).

After an interval of seven years the Revd. Samuel Barton was appointed by the Bishop of London and he described himself as 'Preacher to the Factory at Oporto'. The original of his Subscription to the Bishops Register is lodged in the Guildhall Library and, translated from the Latin, reads 'April 13th 1682, I Samuel Barton B. Th. to be inducted to preach the word of God in the City of Oporto in Portugal, gladly and sincerely subscribe to these three Articles set out above and to all that is contained therein'.

Although the Treaty of 1654 had given the British the privilege of holding services unobtrusively in private houses, this right was not respected and Barton, who had evidently attracted unfavourable attention from the Inquisition, was expelled in 1683. On his return to London, he wrote a report about the circumstances of his expulsion to Dr. Francis Turner, Chaplain to the Bishop of London. The original of this report is in the Public Record Office, Ref. SP 89/15 f. 115/6, and a copy is on view in the Factory House.

Barton had written: 'Quickly after my arrival I began to exercise my function duly every Sunday according to the order prescribed by the Church of England, privately in the same house, the whole Factory commonly

Chapter 2

resorting thither except four who before my coming had revolted to the Church of Rome'. Barton appealed against his expulsion and the Factory members wrote to the British Envoy in Lisbon, asking for his assistance in the matter. But it was of no avail. 'Within three weeks or a month after my Petition had been sent to Lisbon, I was again sent for by the Chancellor who told me my Petition had been presented to the Prince, but he did not think fit to grant it, but continued his command that I should embarque from Oporto by the next ship'. Barton was very reluctant to embark at Oporto as the vessels sailing from there were very small and in danger of being attacked by the 'Sallee Rovers' pirates based at Salé, near Rabat in Morocco, who would attack any ships in the Atlantic that promised easy prey. He petitioned that he might be allowed to sail in a larger ship from Lisbon, which would be better protected, but to no avail, and he was taken on board the British ship 'Palmtree', 'late in the night and the next morning we came over the Barre'.

The Prince Regent was obviously acting under great pressure and the incident shows clearly that the Crown had little influence over the Inquisition However in correspondence with Charles II, who had expressed his resentment at the treatment of the British merchants in Oporto, the Prince was said to be in 'a great passion' over Barton's expulsion.

Charles II had married Catherine of Braganza, thus being brother-in-law to the Prince Regent, who had become King D. Pedro II in 1683. The far-reaching privileges that had been granted to the British merchants under the 1654 Treaty were resented by the local authorities. The latter, encouraged by the Inquisition, summoned the new Factory Minister and obliged him to sign a paper stating he would never preach or exercise the religion of the Church of England. The Inquisition claimed that a priest was not essential to Protestant worship and the British Envoy in Lisbon went so far as to produce the Anglican Book of Common Prayer to prove that this was not the case.

The expulsion of Barton was all the more remarkable because even earlier than the 1654 Treaty the British were said to have been permitted the free exercise of their religion, without interference from the Inquisition, under an Agreement between Charles I and King D. João IV in 1640. However this Treaty, if it actually was signed, was certainly not considered valid by the Portuguese religious authorities as otherwise the British would surely have brought out Chaplains to the Lisbon and Oporto Factories at an earlier date than they did.

An interesting point in the letter from Barton was that at a time when mos of the merchants were without doubt of Anglican or low-church persuasion, yet four of the Factory had been converted to Rome, Barton implying that he arrived too late to prevent this. Consul Maynard in 1683 even went so far as to name the Oporto merchants who had become Roman Catholics.

In the numerous official despatches arising from the Barton affair, Consul Maynard wrote to the Foreign Secretary in London in 1682 'No man knew better than my selfe that King John the 4th did grant us the free exercise of our Religion in Portugal and told me after he had ratified the Treaty that we should doe to give noe scandal to his subjects but have our meetings as privately as we could'. This would hardly refer to any Treaty in 1640, many years before Maynard was appointed to Lisbon.

In 1684 Fanshawe had written from Lisbon that 'the English in Oporto had been very indiscreet about their Burials lately. Previously they had been conducted privately'. This may provide the clue to Barton's expulsion.

The Factory House at Oporto

The furore over Barton evidently continued for some years, as four years after his expulsion the matter was taken to the Privy Council in London in 1687 and presumably the close personal relationship between the two royal families helped to preserve the independence and privileges enjoyed by the British in Portugal. Barton himself did not return, but a new Minister was soon to replace him.

One source has given the date of the foundation of the Lisbon Factory as 1658, but in an earlier reference in the State Papers (P.R.O.) it is recorded that Charles I appointed John Howe as Consul-General in Lisbon and in 1633 gave him 'full power and authority to govern our merchants and to assist them, their factors, agents and servants'. Howe was possibly the first Consul in Lisbon chosen and appointed from London.

A later document in 1660 records a petition from the merchants in Lisbon to Charles II protesting against the Consul-General Thos. Maynard who had been appointed in 1656 by Cromwell to 'Lisbon and other Chief Ports in the Kingdom'. It was described as a 'Humble Petition of the merchants trading with the Kingdom of Portugal and the Factory residing in the City of Lisbon'.

Nearly a century later, the British Envoy, Castres, reported, after the earthquake of 1755, that 'our poor Factory, from a very opulent one, is totally ruined'.

Maynard had also been given powers to appoint in all or any of the ports 'fit and sufficient persons to be Deputy Consuls'. For Oporto, he did not look beyond his own family and in 1659 nominated his brother Walter as Vice-Consul. The latter, in 1661, sent a despatch to the Secretary of State in London with a request that 'The Minister that is to be sent over to this Factory, that he may be an able orthodox divine, for we have too many fanaticks amongst us already'.

During this period there appear to have been constant quarrels between the Consul in Lisbon and the Factories in Lisbon and Oporto, and eventually the latter were successful in having Thos. Maynard removed. Matters came to a head when he tried to dismiss the Vice-Consul Murcot because he had become a Roman Catholic, and the Oporto Factory refused to accept any substitute. Maynard wrote to London 'so ignorant are these young men the Factors as to suffer themselves to be imposed on by those that are fallen off to the Church of Rome'.

However, the 'young men' defeated Maynard and kept their Vice-Consul, whose services as a Portuguese translator were highly valued.

The incident emphasises the independence enjoyed by the Factory merchants and their power over the Consul-General. It is probable that Maynard, who had been appointed by Cromwell and was in ecclesiastical terms a dissenter or very low-church Protestant, exceeded the powers conferred on him by his patent, because there is no doubt that the merchants were at that time entitled to select their own Vice-Consul. Maynard allowed his religious bias to influence his better judgement, but he was soon forced to retract under the threat of the non-payment of his fees by the merchants, and he received little response to his numerous reports to London in 1683 on the subject, including one that even accused Murcot of converting money to his own use that had been collected for poor seamen.

[11]

A
CATALOGUE
Of SEVENTEEN PIPES of excellent
RED PORT WINE,
Of the YEAR 1769,

A N D

Eight Hogfheads of remarkable fine high flavour'd
CLARET;

Which will be SOLD by AUCTION,

By Mr. CHRISTIE,

At his Great Room, next *Cumberland Houfe*, *Pall Mall*,

On *Thurfday*, December 8, 1774, at Two o'Clock.

The faid WINES are perfectly GENUINE, of fingular Quality, and may
be tafted till the Sale.

The Factory House at Oporto

3

No evidence of previous Factory House ☆ Date of formation of Factory in Oporto ☆ Premises used by the Consul & Merchants ☆ The new street of S. João ☆ Demolition of buildings ☆ John Whitehead and John Carr ☆ The building of the Santo António Hospital ☆ Architectural changes in Oporto

In this early period, the second half of the 17th century, there are no clear references to any house being used by the Factory in Oporto as their headquarters. In Consul Crispin's report in 1830, discussed in more detail later, he mentions a house or houses being used by the Factory in the early 18th century, but evidence, admittedly not conclusive, from the correspondence referred to earlier and dated 1703 and 1704 from Thomas Woodmass to his father in England, describing his visit to the north of Portugal, tends to discount the existence of any 'house' at that date. He was received by Consul Lee in 'a tavern in the Rua Nuovo'. Although some of the rooms of the Factory House were a century later to be used as an inn for travellers, it seems unlikely that Woodmass could have confused any previous 'house' being used by the Factory or by the Consul with a tavern. Perhaps Woodmass was considered too unimportant a visitor even to be received at the Consulate if such existed.

But the evidence of this and subsequent travellers visiting Oporto must be treated with caution, as so often their visits were of short duration and their impressions extremely superficial.

A later writer, Arthur Costigan in *Sketches of Society and Manners in Portugal* (1787), described in great detail his visit to Oporto in 1779, with special reference to John Whitehead in whose house he stayed, but he gave no mention or hint that any previous Factory House existed.

Another writer of the same period, Agostinho Rebello da Costa, in *Descripção Topográfica e Histórica da Cidade do Porto* (1789), gave details of the building of the Factory House, described as still uncompleted at that date and on which 150 workmen were engaged. He estimated that the total cost would amount to 200,000 cruzados, the equivalent then of about £17,700. No mention was made by this writer of any previous Factory House nor is any such House to be found in an engraving of the city of Oporto from a drawing by Teodoro Maldonado, a well-known Oporto architect who was a contemporary and collaborator of John Whitehead. This drawing was made probably between 1775 and 1780 and shows the new Santo António Hospital, the building of which had started in 1770. Maldonado would certainly have included any previous Factory House if such had existed.

Nearly 40 years later, in 1825, the signatories to a Memorial sent to the Foreign Secretary, in which they were claiming for all British subjects equal rights to the Factory House, made no mention of any previous House. One of

Contemporary cartoon of John Croft Esq. of York, member of the Factory at Oporto

John Croft Esq.ʳ York, Member of the Factory at Oporto,S.S.AS. & Free of the Cities of Edinborough and York &c &c

the witnesses to this Memorial was one Manuel Moreira da Silva, described as 'late Master Carpenter ninety years of age more or less'. He declared that he had perfect knowledge of the Factory House 'constructed by him in the capacity of Master Carpenter'. He made no reference to any house demolished on the same site, nor of any building there previously that had been used by the Factory. Similarly Murphy who was in Oporto in 1789 and who wrote about the Factory House when it was nearly completed, never mentioned that it was replacing any previous House.

There is therefore little contemporary evidence in the matter, in the absence of any categorical statement as to whether a previous House ever existed or not.

The Factory House at Oporto

However, over thirty years later, the members of the Factory sent a representation to George Canning, then Foreign Secretary, in which they said, 'in and before the year 1765 the Factory possessed certain plots of land with a house which was pulled down previous to the erection of that which now exists. In 1767 the Factory purchased a small plot of ground which was necessary to complete the site of the present House. It was purchased by John Whitehead Consul and the Merchants of the Factory'.

A few years later, in 1830, Consul Crispin was to report 'the Factory possessed houses and premises so distant back as 1710 . . . it would be vain to enter into a great deal of minutiae describing the purposes to which the Factory House was at first appropriated or intended when rebuilt, whether for business, amusement, accomodation (sic) or hilarity'.

Crispin, writing of events that had taken place about half a century ago, was not entirely correct in his statement about the earlier houses. It was in fact Consul Lee who was known to have purchased for himself a house in the Rua Nova in 1710, and this was sold by his widow in 1729 and later in 1771 bought back by Consul Whitehead and the merchants. It is logical to assume that this house was used by the Factory for meetings.

We are therefore left with rather scanty evidence, which can be interpreted in one way or another. Either the premises used by the Factory belonged to the Consul or merchants or both, or else they owned collectively what must have been an extremely small house with some plots of land. In the latter case it is remarkable that the house was never shown on contemporary maps of the period.

In documents in the 17th century it was usual to refer to the 'Oporto Factory', but in 1710, in a despatch to London, Consul Milner reported from Lisbon that the 'Port Factory' protested against the heavy duties imposed upon all wines. This description may either have been a reference to those members of the Factory who were port shippers, or more likely it is an indication that even at that early date the membership of the Factory consisted exclusively of port shippers. It is surprising however that the shippers should have complained at that time, as the Methuen Treaty of 1703 had secured for them preferential tariffs on their wines entering Britain, although it is true to say that the benefits of the Treaty were not reflected in increased sales until some years later. But sweet Lisbon wines were shipped in greater quantities as a result of the Treaty.

At an earlier date, in 1673, Captain James Jenifer of the vessel *Saudades* had written a journal of his voyage to Lisbon, in which he strongly criticised the foreign merchants in Portugal, especially the English, 'who have been very successful in gaining estates, but how honestly I cannot determine'. He gave a list of merchants in Oporto, headed by Vice-Consul Walter Maynard, but the names are not easily identified as being those of wine shippers, although one, John Cooke, was in 1683 the writer of a letter on behalf of the Factory to Consul Thomas Maynard in Lisbon protesting at the removal of Vice-Consul Edward Murcot and stating that the Factory would not allow interference from Maynard. The same year Maynard complained to London that 'the Merchants of the Factory at Oporto had not paid his salary because I displaced their Vice-Consul and they refuse to receive any other that I nominate'.

Another mention by Jenifer was of Samuel Maddox whose imprisonment, with seizure of his books, had caused such a furore, with much

[15]

Portrait of Consul John Whitehead

The Factory House at Oporto

correspondence in 1675 and 1676 from the Minister in Lisbon, Francis Parry, to the Secretary of State in London and to the 'English Factory at Oporto'.

Various writers attributed different dates to the formation of the Oporto Factory and Consul Crispin in his report dated 6th October 1830 to the Foreign Office, 'Relating to the Factory House at Oporto', wrote 'The Factory at Oporto, considered as a body of British Merchants, may be traced to the close of 1600 or the early part of 1700'. It is curious that he had not seen the Consular reports relating to the Factory many years earlier and that he was apparently unaware that the first Chaplain to the Factory, the Revd. John Brawlerd, had been appointed in 1671.

Crispin also reported that 'early in 1700 there were already several permanent houses of business and in 1727 they had so much augmented as to form in that year a code of Rules and Regulations for their guidance as the British Factory'. John Croft in *A Treatise on the Wines of Portugal* (1788) reported 'The British Merchants or Factors at Oporto in a manner incorporated themselves and made certain rules for their proceedings'. This date, 1727, has on the strength of these statements been interpreted by various writers as marking the origin and foundation of the British Factory at Oporto. This is clearly incorrect and whereas Crispin may well have been right, to the extent that the Factory Members decided in that year that they needed a better organisation and a more regulated constitution, yet it can hardly provide proof, in the face of so much evidence to the contrary, that the Factory did not exist earlier.

In 1763 the Oporto Town Council decided to make a new street to be called Rua S. João, which was to connect the river front at the Ribeira, cutting across the street which had been made three centuries earlier in the reign of D. João I and called at first Rua Nova then Rua Formosa* then again Rua Nova dos Inglezes, or sometimes just Rua dos Inglezes, and finally by the present name Rua Infante D. Henrique.

The Council had in fact petitioned in 1763 for permission to make the new street, but only in 1765 was the request granted by Royal Decree.

Crispin reported that 'The Municipality intending to cut a new street contiguous to it, purchased among other houses to be razed one that is described in the deed of sale as "parting on the northern side with the courtyard and garden of the Factory House".' Crispin continued that 'Consul Whitehead and the members of the Factory purchased of the Municipality part of these very premises and part were given in return for what was taken belonging to the Factory to form the line of the new street. The title deeds expressed that it was ceded in perpetuity by the Municipality to Consul Whitehead and the merchants of the Factory then resident and to those that might come hereafter'.

A copy of the original document signed on this occasion, in the possession of the British Association, makes it clear that Crispin was not correct in stating that any premises were actually bought by Whitehead and the 'business men of the Factory'. Any property they may have occupied was most certainly held on a lease. The agreement made on this occasion by Whitehead involved a very small area of land, and writers who had claimed that the subsequent conversion of the whole Factory House site to freehold about eighty years later was granted by the Queen of Portugal in compensation for what had

[17]   *Pinho Leal, Vol. 6, p. 57.

Chapter 3

Letter from Robert Porrett to the Secretary of State, Henry Fox, declining the appointment as Consul at Oporto (P.R.O. SP 89/50 No. 296)

296

I can't in justice to Our Factory omitt telling Your Lordship, that they behaved extremely handsome on the occasion, as well in regard to the memory of the Deceased, as to myself; they all refusing to give their Votes to any one, till they were satisfyed I declined it; But upon my relinquishing it they made choice of Mr. John Whitehead

I most sincerely wish your Lordship, all imaginable Success & Satisfaction in the Administration of your High Office, I am with the greatest Respect & Submission

My Lord

Your Lordships

Most Obedient

& most Devoted

humble Servant

Porto 6th August 1756

Robert Porrett

Letter from John Whitehead to the Secretary of State, Henry Fox, accepting the appointment as Consul (P.R.O. SP 89/50 No. 297)

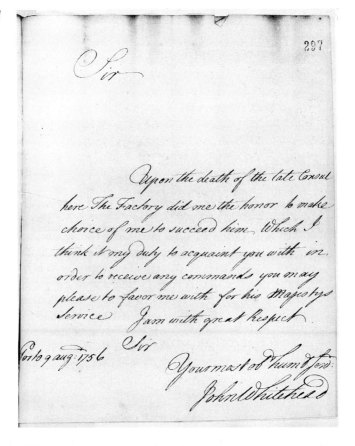

297

Sir

Upon the death of the late Consul here The Factory did me the honor to make choice of me to succeed him, Which I think it my duty to acquaint you with in order to receive any commands you may please to favor me with for his Majestys Service I am with great Respect

Sir

Porto 9 aug: 1756

Your most ob humb Serv:

John Whitehead

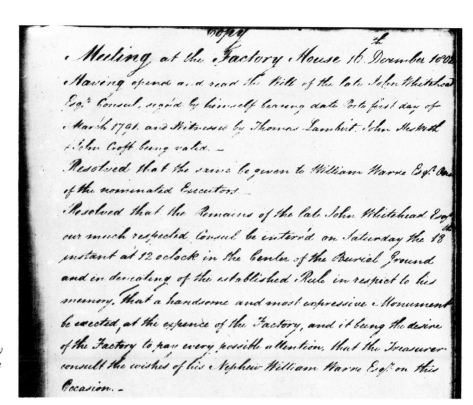

The opening of the minutes of the meeting at the Factory House in 1802 following the death of Consul Whitehead (P.R.O. FO 63/40)

been taken from the Factory to widen the new street were clearly wrong. Such theories take no account of the considerable interval between the two events.

John Whitehead has already been mentioned and he will continue to play an important part in this story. He was born in 1726 at Ashton-under-Lyne near Manchester, the son of Thomas Whitehead. The previous Consul in Oporto, Robert Jackson, died on 6th August 1756 and the post was offered by the Factory to his son-in-law, Robert Porrett, but he declined it and the Factory then elected John Whitehead. He must have been in Oporto at the time because on 9th August 1756 he notified his election as Consul to Henry Fox, the Secretary of State in London. This confirms that the members of the Factory were able to nominate the Consul without any prior reference to the Foreign Office.

It was fortunate for the Factory and the Port Wine trade that Jackson's son-in-law declined the nomination. If he had accepted, it is very likely that the Factory House would never have been built.

Whitehead was to remain in Oporto until his death in December 1802. It is certain that his election by the Factory was due to a recommendation from his brother-in-law, William Warre, one of the leading members of the British Community, who had married Whitehead's sister Elizabeth in 1745. He was not a 'career' Consul and there is no evidence in Foreign Office records that he held any previous consular appointment.

Costigan was the only writer of the period to make more than a passing reference to Whitehead. He stayed with him in Oporto on two occasions in 1778 and 1779 and they made several excursions together to various provincial towns. He wrote: 'This Consul our landlord here is a most uncommon character and when young had been it seems also initiated in the mysteries of trade and had begun in perhaps as fair a line of business as any other young man in London. But the attractions of a life of dissipation in that metropolis had more charms for his youth and when he came to reflect a little the universality of his genius was not to be limited by the trammels of commerce, of which he retained only what is necessary for executing the office of Consul and at the same time that he discharged it with all the punctuality and care of a man of honour, it leaves him sufficient time to follow the bent of his own natural genius and inclination'.

Whitehead was described as living in a very large house with no Counting-House nor a family to mind and though far enough from being a young man he was still a bachelor. His height was given as 5ft. 7ins. and he usually wore a wig and brown coat.

From the records of the British Church we learn that his house, in 1785, was in Rua de São Francisco. This street still exists and lies near and to the west of Rua Infante D. Henrique (formerly Rua Nova dos Inglezes) and thus only a short walk from the Factory House.

Whitehead's domestics, according to Costigan, 'consist of a withered old Portuguese beldam, past eighty, who makes his bed, lights his fire and sends him in his breakfast and a young Galician boy who cleans his shoes and brings him a powdered wig once or twice every day from the nearest barbers shop'.

Of the house itself, 'his library consists of a large and heterogeneous collection of books. In another room adjoining the library stands a pair of the largest globes I have yet seen . . . these have been lately finished here under his own direction. From his library you ascend by a spacious staircase to a platform covered with lead which serves him for an observatory'.

For another mention of Whitehead, James Murphy in his *Journal* described him as a gentleman from whom he received the kindest and most hospitable attentions and spoke in the highest terms of his accomplishments and taste for the fine arts.

'The Portuguese according to their custom of translating into their own language the names of foreigners styled him Cabeça Branca (i.e. White Head)'. Murphy also mentioned his library as being extensive but ill-arranged.

The contract for the leasehold was not signed personally by Whitehead or by the members of the Factory as they had given a Power of Attorney to their representative the Reverend Doctor João Batista de Carvalho. The members of the Factory mentioned as signatories to the Power of Attorney were, apart from John Whitehead, John Olive, a partner in the firm Holdsworth, Olive and Newman (subsequently Hunt Roope & Co.), Thomas Stafford of the firms Dawson Stafford and Stafford Cooper, mentioned later in connection with the British Cemetery, Charles Page of Noble & Murat, George Wye of John & George Wye & Co., and Wm. Calvert of Warre & Co., all these being wine shippers. The remaining two, William Jensen and James Alvey cannot be identified with any wine firms, although a John Alvey was mentioned in connection with the British Hospital for several years from 1812.

The above contract refers to premises situated on the side of the present Factory House facing Rua S. João. There are also references to three houses, most probably on the frontage of the present House, said to have been in the possession of the British merchants for residential and club purposes and to have been demolished in 1786 to make room for the new building. While this is the year most usually given as the date the building of the Factory House commenced, yet some sources give the more precise date one year earlier, 28th February 1785.

It must be remembered that the district round the Rua Nova dos Inglezes, as it was then called, in which the Factory House lies, was at that time the main residential and commercial area of the city and many of the British merchants had offices there, as well as private houses nearby. Some of these were certainly used for Factory meetings and social gatherings in the same way as in Lisbon the Consul's house or that of one of the Factory members were used for their meetings.

Kingston in 1845 described the Rua Nova dos Inglezes as 'of no great length, but the broadest in the city and contains some good houses. Here the merchants hold their exchange and congregate to talk business or the last new opera'.

Costigan also mentioned the street. 'To walk much about this city is, I assure you, rather a violent exercise, not one street in it being upon a level excepting that where the most part of the English inhabit'.

The colloquial name given to the Rua dos Inglezes was Praca do Commércio, (Pinho Leal Vol. 6 pp. 57/8), for the British merchants met there to transact business. Another writer, (J.A. Pinto Ferreira *O Vinho na História Portuguesa* Sec. XIII-XIX, 1982, p. 274) mentioned that the British Factory frequented a Café in Praça do Commércio in the 18th century. Possibly this was the tavern where Thomas Woodmass was received by the Consul, as related earlier.

Whatever buildings existed on the site of the Factory House, they must have been of extremely modest dimensions compared with the grandiose designs planned by John Whitehead. His original plans have not survived and there is no means of knowing over what period of time he had formed the concept of the new building, but it must have been under consideration for many years, if only to allow for sufficient funds to be raised to finance the scheme. It was clearly a very personal ambition on the part of Whitehead to design the building, as otherwise he could easily have entrusted it to his friend John Carr (1723–1807), a distinguished Yorkshire architect who was born at Horbury, near Wakefield, and twice mayor of York. Carr, on Whitehead's recommendation, had been commissioned by the Oporto authorities, headed by Governor João de Almada, to submit designs for the new Santo António Hospital in Oporto. In this connection, one source stated that Whitehead and the British Chaplain, the Reverend Henry Wood, helped in the negotiations between Carr and the Hospital board. The Chaplain was an ancestor of the Earl of Halifax (Viceroy of India 1926–31 and Foreign Secretary 1938–40) and a photograph of his portrait, presented by Lord Halifax after his visit to the Factory House in 1951, hangs in the Map Room.

Even if Wood was not actually instrumental in helping Carr to obtain acceptance for his designs, he certainly acted as an intermediary in the matter. Carr wrote a letter to the President of the Hospital Board in Oporto, D. António de Lancastre, dated 7th August 1769 from York, in which he acknowledged the latter's instructions to send out his designs: 'I very much lament my being prevented the honour of corresponding with your Lordship on this important Subject, by Dr. Wood not aquainting (sic) me in due time

Rua dos Inglezes, Oporto; a photograph of c.1880

with Your Instructions to Dr. Wood in March or April last, those instructions by reason I believe of Dr. Wood's indisposition were not communicated to me until 20th July at which time I had completed my design and waited with impatience to be informed how I might send the design to Your Lordship. Fortunately Dr. Wood arrived in this city yesterday, on account of his health, and an opportunity now offers by which I can send Your Lordship the drawings immediately by Capt. Sconswar who I have impowered to receive i ... a design which the King of England has seen with admiration and approbation. He desired to see it, having heard so great an account of it and of the Noble Founder D. António de Lancaster (sic) from a great many noblemen of my acquaintance'. This was a reference to Carr's many titled and influential patrons including the Marquis of Rockingham, for whom Carr was engaged on work at Wentworth Woodhouse, and the Duke of Devonshire and many others. In fact Rockingham wrote to Carr in 1779 about the hospital plans in terms that revealed a close friendship: 'I much wish your letter had brought me a satisfactory account of the state of your health. If it was not time of war I should almost recommend to you a sea voyage to a warm climate. I don't know whether the grand plan you sent to Lisbon has been carried into execution, it might do you good to go and look. I am Ever, Dear Carr, your affectionate friend Rockingham.'* However it seems that Carr never went abroad to Portugal or to any other country.

He concluded his letter to the Hospital by referring to 'many magnificent

*Wentworth Woodhouse Muniments, Rockingham letters.

The Factory House at Oporto

Structures that I am conducting for several Noblemen and others in the Kingdom. . . . Be pleased to give me leave most Noble Lord to observe that I shall be very sorry to anticipate Your Lordship's generosity by setting you a price upon this extensive Plan, yet in justice to my experience and abilities in architecture and the esteem and reward which I receive for my designs in England, make it necessary perhaps for me to inform Your Lordship that £500 would be thought but a very moderate reward for such a design in England . . . I shall not ask more of Your Lordship than the above sum of £500, which sum I desire Your Lordship will remit me by my acquaintance Captain Robert Sconswar who is a man of Credit'.*

At the time Carr wrote this letter, Henry Wood had relinquished his appointment as Chaplain in Oporto and therefore was not available to take Carr's designs back there.

The designs were accepted and the foundation stone of the hospital was laid on 10th June 1770 and building continued until 1780 when it was suspended due to lack of funds. In the meantime Carr, who was certainly kept informed by John Whitehead of the progress that was being made, complained about alterations to his designs on the part of the builders. Work started again in 1791 and the first patients were admitted in 1799. Work went on intermittently for nearly half a century and was finally discontinued in 1843. The building was never completed on the scale envisaged by Carr, only the main frontage and half the length of the two sides being finished. Nevertheless it remains a very fine building and certainly one of the most imposing in Oporto.

However, two British writers were distinctly pessimistic about it. Costigan described a walk around Oporto with John Whitehead in 1779: 'We arrived at a new and very extensive building, not much more than begun; it was to consist of a square of above 560 English feet each front. The Consul led us into a small house adjoining and shewed us the plans, profiles and elevations, which he said had been designed by an architect, an old schoolfellow of his own in England and had been examined by His Majesty the King of Great Britain who he said was an excellent judge: that it was intended for a General Hospital but was an undertaking much too immense for such a place as this and would better serve the purpose of a General Infirmary for London or Lisbon. That in the little of it which was executed they had already departed very materially from the original design and made many alterations for the worse: that the fund assigned for carrying it on did not afford above a thousand pounds sterling yearly and that there was no great danger of it ever being finished while Portugal remained in its present precarious situation, for that the whole estimate of the expense had been laid at about 300,000 pounds sterling'.

Murphy in 1790 was also of the same opinion: 'The Great Hospital if completed would be the largest building in Oporto. Although it is upwards of twenty years since the foundation of this structure was laid, there is yet but a wing of one of the pavilions covered in; the rest is raised but a few feet above the surface and is likely to remain in this state, a magnificent modern ruin and a lasting monument of the folly of not proportioning the design to the public purse'.

An interesting sequel was that in 1793 the original designs made by Carr

*Records of Santa Casa da Misericordia, Oporto.

Chapter 3

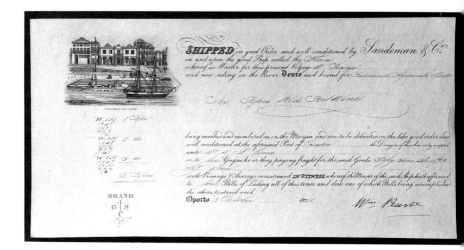

Bill of Lading dated 1851 depicting a view of Sandeman's lodges

were said to have deteriorated to such an extent that Joaquim da Costa Lima Sampaio was instructed to make copies of them, the respective Minute at the hospital saying 'owing to the skill he had acquired in the house of the English Consul who had made use of his services'. This can be taken as an indication that he was, at least to some extent, responsible for the building of the Factory House under Whitehead's direction.

It is of course possible that Carr may have given advice to Whitehead with regard to his design for the Factory House and a comment in *Portuguese Architecture*, Walter Crum Watson, London 1908, considers that 'the plans of both (i.e. the Hospital and the Factory House) have clearly been sent out from England, the Hospital especially being thoroughly English in design'. That is tantamount to suggesting that in fact the plans for the Factory House were drawn up by Carr himself, but this is unlikely. In many respects the design of the Factory House could also be described as thoroughly English, notably the central circular staircase with wrought iron balustrade and lighting from the top, features which had become fashionable in English houses in the middle of the 18th century, and also the arrangement of the communicating reception rooms on the principal floor which was clearly designed for the entertainments in vogue at that time, in particular the balls, receptions and card playing. Whitehead was certainly influenced by the current trends in style and design of English houses both town and country at that period.

The same Costa Lima Sampaio, who will also be mentioned later in connection with the building of the British Chapel in 1815, was responsible for the design of the house in Oporto that was subsequently the Royal Palace. Built in 1795 for two brothers of the Moraes e Castro family (Barons of Nevogilde), it was sold by one of their descendants to King D. Pedro V in 1861, and later became the *Museu Nacional Soares dos Reis*. Sampaio may also have been the architect of the Sandeman Lodges in Vila Nova de Gaia. The façade of these, facing the River Douro, includes a loggia with five arches and a single upper storey with a small central pediment. The date of construction has been put by one source as 1797, but the firm itself has no documentary evidence to support this. An interesting drawing of their Lodges appears on the Bills of Lading used by the firm in the nineteenth century. One of these dated 1851 is illustrated above. It was said to have been designed and drawn by Edwin Sandeman, third son of the Founder George Sandeman.

The Factory House at Oporto

These and subsequent buildings in the early 19th century, notably the Palâcio da Bolsa and the University, continued to reflect the departure from the Italian baroque that had dominated the architecture of Oporto under the influence of the Tuscan Nicolau Nasoni, in favour of the Palladian style first introduced from England by John Carr with his grand design for the Hospital and, certainly under his guidance, by John Whitehead and his pupil Sampaio.

The Factory House was evidently much admired by most visitors to Oporto, though one writer, James Murphy, was not impressed. He wrote in *Travels in Portugal* (1795) that 'of Whitehead's Factory at Oporto very little can be said, being in the anti-Moorish style, like all the modern works of architecture in this country'.

It has been claimed that the Factory House in Oporto is the last surviving building of this name in the world, and this is undoubtedly true. At the same time it is open to question whether any other Factory Houses built in such a style and for purely social purposes ever actually existed in other countries.

It can safely be assumed that if John Whitehead had not been Consul in Oporto at that time and the possessor of great creative architectural talent, not to mention his reputation and influence with the local authorities and in particular the Governor João de Almada, no Factory House would ever have been built and, on the abolition of foreign factories in Portugal in 1810, the British Factory in Oporto would gradually have died away and the British Association never have been founded.

Part of a page of Christie catalogue of 22nd February 1810

A

CATALOGUE,

&c. &c. &c.

THURSDAY, the 22d of FEBRUARY, 1810,

Old Port.

1   THREE dozen of capital Old Port, Vintage 1790, at per dozen,
bottles included   ———   Bin No. 7

2 Ditto

4

The missing Factory records

After the building was completed in 1790, and all writers on the subject agree on this date, no records appear to exist until 1804, when the whole property was included in one lease from the Crown. According to Consul Crispin 'the possessors of all property held of the Crown were in 1802 called upon to produce their Title Deeds and amongst them Consul Whitehead. This led to a long proceeding and they were not to be found'.

If this is correct, it is in contradiction to the subsequent report that all the archives including the Title Deeds were taken to England by Consul Warre in 1807*. According to the Foreign Office lists, William Warre was Consul from 1805 until 1812. This is not correct because, as already related, he was appointed in 1802 by the Factory. He does not in fact appear to have returned to Oporto after the French occupation and significantly he was not mentioned among those members who gave the Ball in June 1811 to mark the re-occupation of the Factory House.

The next Consul, John Crispin, was requested in 1814 by the Factory members 'to write to William Warre in England on the subject of the Title Deeds of the House in the Rua Nova dos Inglezes and that should he possess these deeds, to beg he will send them over by some careful conveyance, reserving legal copies in his possession which he will have drawn up in English'. There is no record as to whether this request ever reached Warre.

Subsequent to Warre's death Consul Crispin reported that the Minister of State called upon the relatives of Consul Warre in England to produce the Oporto Factory records. This apparently they did not do and the Foreign Office records mentioned that 'afterwards they could not be found'.

It is interesting that the Lisbon Factory experienced the same problem over their Journals for the period 1749–1807, which were said to have been taken to England in 1807 by Consul-General James Gambier and never heard of again.

The conclusion is inevitably reached that Consul Warre only took to England records concerning the Church and not those of the Factory. This is the simple explanation of all the speculation and doubt that has always existed, the more so as Crispin had not specifically mentioned Title Deeds as being taken to England, but only 'Books & Papers'.

This view is confirmed by a Minute of a meeting of the British Association on 24th June 1824 at which 'The Treasurer was requested to lay on the table the Title Deeds of the Factory House, which were opened and read'.

Similarly, on the 19th May 1830, 'it was resolved that the Title Deeds, policy of assurance and certain papers relating to the Factory House be sealed up and delivered to Mr. Roope to deposit in his iron safe, which was done

*Ref. Foreign Office Records.

The Factory House at Oporto

accordingly'. The insurance policy, dated 1825, has survived and is hung in the Map Room.

Then two years later on 26th September 1832, the Treasurer Arthur Hunt wrote to the Secretary of State in London enclosing an opinion, on the subject of the exclusive right to the Factory House, of two Portuguese lawyers 'To whom the British Association submitted the title deeds'.*

The Church records taken to England by William Warre are preserved in the Guildhall Library in the City of London, Foreign Register Section. They include the *Memoranda Book of the British Factory at Oporto, recording baptisms 1717-20 and 1723-89, marriages 1716-19, 1723-24 and 1729-97 and burials 1716-18, 1723-25 and 1784-87.*† The book has the general title of *Register of Ye Port Factory*, dated 1716, and the Chaplain, Henry Pakenham, was described as the 'Minister of Ye Factory at Oporto'. The book was also inscribed 'Register of Births, Marriages & Burials of Protestant British subjects at Porto in Portugal, brought from thence by the then Consul at the time of the expulsion of the British subjects from Portugal in November 1807'.

In the same library is the *Register General of the British Factory at Oporto 1788-1865.* **

The author has consulted these records in the hope that they might provide valuable information about the early years of the Oporto Factory, but they are in fact solely Church records.

One reference however, dated 1798, does record the early connection between the Factory and the establishment of the British Cemetery and subsequently with the building of the British Chapel, financed from the Contribution Fund. It is appropriate at this point to give the full story.

*Ref. Foreign Office correspondence (Portuguese (63) Vol. 427). P.R.O.
†Ms. 10,446 A.
**Ms. 10,446 B.

Chapter 4

Factory resolution concerning the Cemetery ☆ The building of the British Chapel

At a meeting of the Factory on 2nd April 1798, the following resolution was passed: 'Resolved that the Graves at the Burying Ground be henceforward dug in sequence from left to right and that a stone of Valongo slate numbered, being two Palmos high (about 18 inches) out of the ground and at the foot of the same a stone one Palmo square out of the ground and that no inscription whatever be allowed to be put on any stone, but the Chaplain to keep a register of the Burials according to the number on the grave stone. The expenses to be paid by this Factory. That the card of the Burying Ground be given to the Chaplain'.

It was also recorded that in consequence of the above Resolution the first stone was placed at the grave of Thomas Stafford, bearing the Mark No. 1, on 4th August 1798. He was the father of Conway Stafford, 'Chaplain of the Factory at Oporto', who was married in 1799 to Isabel Page, the service being taken by the Reverend H. Hill, Chaplain to the British Factory at Lisbon. One of the witnesses was John Croft, who in his *Treatise* of 1788 had described himself as a member of the Factory at Oporto and Wine Merchant of York.

The purchase of the ground for the British Cemetery and for the site where the Chapel was to be built about thirty years later was closely connected with the Factory.

In 1785 Consul John Whitehead was authorised by the local authorities to buy land to build a cemetery for what were described as 'English vassals', with the stipulation that it should be well away from the population and from the walls of the City, to avoid any troubles or inconveniences.

After some other sites had been considered, the present land was bought and the transfer tax paid on 7th June 1785, although due to questions over the measurement of the land the final contract was only signed in January 1787. Apart from Whitehead, there were mentioned in the official documents the following 'British businessmen of the body of the British Factory', Dickson (probably Dixon), Nicholas Land, Francis Bearsley, George Wye and Thomas Stafford. All these were connected with port shipping firms and the last two had been mentioned earlier in 1767 in Factory documents.

The payment for the Church land was made by James Warre, the nephew of John Whitehead, presumably the Factory Treasurer at the time, although the Master Carpenter Manuel Moreira da Silva, who has been mentioned earlier in connection with the building of the Factory House, described how the land for the Chapel and the Cemetery was 'treated for and bought by him with money which the Consul gave him for that purpose taken from the Contributory (sic) Fund'.

There was no building existing on the site except for what was described as a 'Deposit House' (mortuary) which was subsequently rebuilt in 1817.

Prior to the opening of the official British cemetery, burials had taken place in an unofficial and unconsecrated burial ground on the south bank of the River Douro, on a site described as 'Lugar do Cavaco opposite the Bicalho'. This was near, and to the east of, where the modern Arrabida bridge stands. At an earlier date burials were at low tide on the seashore or river bank, but few records have survived prior to 1788 and these did not record where the burials took place.

But the erection of any Protestant place of worship continued to be forbidden for many years and the first indication that the ban had been lifted came at a meeting on 14th December 1814 of the 'British Merchants appointed to manage the Contribution Fund agreeable to Act of Parliament'. On this date the possibility of building a Chapel was first mooted in these terms:

'Resolved unanimously that the propriety of building a Chapel in conformity to the recent Treaty of Commerce, be taken into consideration at the first general meeting in the New Year'. This Minute was signed by the Consul John Crispin and twelve members of the Contribution Fund. (In fact the Treaty was not so recent, having been signed in 1810.)

Accordingly, on 2nd January 1815, it was recorded: 'The propriety of building a Chapel in conformity to the recent Treaty of Commerce having been taken into consideration, Resolved unanimously that a Committee be appointed to draw up a plan & Estimate of the Expenditure and that the Treasurer (John Tyndale) and Mr. Knowsley and Mr. Harris be the Committee for that purpose'.

The Committee prepared their report, and on 5th April 1815 a meeting considered it and resolved that 'The Consul be requested to communicate to His Majesty's Ambassador Extraordinary and Plenipotentiary at the Court of Portugal, the anxious wish of His Majesty's Protestant subjects at Oporto to erect a Chapel in conformity to the privilege granted by the recent Commercial Treaty; and to request the acquiescence of His Excellency towards their carrying so pious and desirable a purpose into execution'.

On 1st June 1815 the Consul presented a letter from the Ambassador, George Canning, 'acquiescing in the laudable intention of His Majesty's Protestant subjects in this City, to erect a Chapel for the regular celebration of Divine Worship'. The Bishop of London had expressed similar sentiments in a letter to the Chaplain.

The Ambassador's letter included this instruction: 'In carrying this design into execution, it will be necessary that they should bear in mind the provision annexed by the Treaty to the permission granted for the building of Protestant Chapels – viz that they should resemble private houses in their external appearance and that the use of bells be not permitted therein for the purpose of publicly announcing the time of Divine Service'. For his part the Bishop of London had expressed himself 'extremely desirous that the place fixed on in this City for the performance of Divine Service shall be exclusively appropriate to that purpose and regularly consecrated'.

The meeting of 1st June 1815 resolved that they should proceed immediately towards erecting the British Protestant Chapel and a sub-committee was formed to report on the most advisable mode of carrying it into effect.

The Chapel sub-committee acted very promptly and on the 9th June 1815 issued their report, which contained, inter alia, the following recommendations: 'That the British Burying Ground appears to be the best

Chapter 5

View of the interior of the British Chapel, 1831, by Joaquim Braga Portuense

indeed the only proper spot for the situation of the Chapel'. Secondly, 'in regard to the Chapel itself, the Committee recommend the large room in the Factory House as a model in proportion and dimensions, but in nothing else'. The last words of their recommendation appear rather ambiguous but the measurements of the Factory House ballroom and the Chapel, in the size in which it was originally built, certainly appear to have been the same and at any rate the width can be verified at the present day as being identical.

The reference to the Factory House ballroom certainly lends strong evidence to the belief that church services were held there prior to the construction of the Chapel. No writer has given definite confirmation of this, but one Chaplain in the 19th century claimed that he had heard from old members of the British Community that 'Divine Services had been held for some years in the Ballroom of the British Factory House'.

It is probable that in fact any such services were only held during the period 1811–18. Prior to the Treaty of 1810, it would have been considered too conspicuous and too provocative to hold services in such a public place.

At the same time, some of the entries in the Contribution Fund cash book in 1814 are very puzzling as these refer to purchases of prayer books, chairs and curtains 'for the Chapel'. It is possible that these items were in fact destined for the room at the Factory House, presumably the ballroom, that was used as a chapel, because there is no record of any other British Chapel having existed unless, following the Treaty of 1810, the Chaplain had furnished a chapel in his or some other private house.

Following their report, the Chapel sub-committee obtained an estimate from the builder 'which he is confident cannot exceed RS. 5200$000 (£1,150) including everything except seats, stoves and blinds'.

The Committee were evidently not aware that the cost of building, even in those days, was liable to prove more expensive than the original estimate, and they went so far as to express the opinion that 'this estimate rather exceeds than falls short of the probable expence (sic)'. They were to be proved very wrong, even allowing for the various alterations they made later to the original plan.

Meanwhile the Chaplain had been requested by the members of the Contribution Fund to ask the Bishop to name a Commission for 'so awful and necessary a Ceremony as the Consecration of the Chapel'. The Bishop regarded this matter as being 'peculiarly difficult of accomplishment since it requires the consent of the Portuguese Government and of the Bishop of the Diocese'. He did not wish to alarm the 'Portuguese Hierarchy'. He felt however that there was no objection to the performance of divine service in an unconsecrated place when the proceedings as in the present instance are justified by necessity. His closing words were a masterpiece of ecclesiastical diplomacy: 'Though I should undoubtedly prefer the sanction of this awful and important ceremony if it can be obtained consistently with the respect which is due to the Law and usages of the Country, the omission not proceeding from negligence will carry its own excuse with it'.

If the building of the Chapel was permitted under Portuguese law since the Treaty of 1810 it is not easily apparent why the Bishop was so apprehensive over possible local opposition, and why the consent of the Portuguese authorities could not be obtained without any difficulty.

From the surviving records, we can establish that work on the construction of the Chapel started on Monday the 19th June 1815, the day on which the Battle of Waterloo ended.

The wage sheet described as '1st Account' shows that twenty stonemasons and general workers were employed, at a maximum wage of 2s. per day, under the direction of Joaquim da Costa Lima Sampaio, who has been mentioned earlier in connection with the Royal Palace and the Hospital in Oporto. He was known to have been a pupil of John Whitehead and most certainly directed the building of the Factory House under Whitehead. He has also been mentioned earlier in connection with the Santo António Hospital.

By the end of 1815, the outside walls of the Chapel must have been nearing completion, as in December of that year four carpenters were employed and the total amount spent so far was about £500. The master carpenter was Jozé Lopez Martins, not the same as was employed in the building of the Factory House, the latter, Manuel Moreira da Silva evidently having retired, being about eighty years of age.

In July 1816 the committee appointed to superintend the building of the

Chapter 5

Chapel were obliged to issue a second report in which it was revealed that the original estimate had proved far too low and it was now thought that the eventual cost would be nearly double at Rs. 10.000$000, the equivalent of about £2,200. The first estimate from the builder had been Rs. 5200$000 'for the rough building' and the Committee had added Rs. 1000$000 for the interior. But all this had been spent, owing partly 'to the nature of the ground in which the foundation was laid, the workmen having unexpectedly dug into the Quarry from whence the stones for the walls of the Burying ground were taken'.

The work was then held up pending a solution as to how the extra cost was to be financed and in November 1816 a meeting of the Contribution Fund decided to sell their holding in England of £3,661 3 per cent Consols and to transfer the proceeds (£2,412) to Oporto. It is therefore quite certain that the total cost of building the Chapel was defrayed from the Contribution Fund and not, as some writers have stated, from any individual subscriptions.

From a study of the accounts that were paid to the builders, carpenters and glazier, it can be definitely established that the Chapel was completed by the end of 1818 and that the total cost amounted to Rs. 13685$000, the equivalent of £3,040.

The interior stucco work was done in 1817 by António Alves Bezerra. The windows were completed in May 1818, but these were only in plain glass and it was not until 1905 that any stained glass windows were put in. The stone for the font was brought from Lisbon in 1830, an item paid for 'cutting the Font' being recorded in 1831.

The Chapel was not consecrated until the 20th August 1843 when the first Bishop of Gibraltar, George Tomlinson, visited.Oporto. Until that date all the records referred to the British Chapel but the Bishop stated that 'the Chapel when consecrated is intended to be called by the name of Saint James', and subsequently the title used was the British Episcopal Church of St. James, or at times during the period 1825–75, the British Church Establishment, this being the official Foreign Office term for Anglican churches abroad, when grants for their upkeep were made by the British Government. The inclusion of 'Episcopal' in the title of the Church continued into this century and the last mention is found in 1929.

At least until 1825 the Chaplains were selected by the Factory and confirmed in their appointment by the Crown. In 1813 the Foreign Secretary Lord Castlereagh wrote from 'Our Court at Carlton House' to the Reverend Richard Pennell saying that 'he having been humbly recommended unto us by the principal merchants settled at Oporto to be Chaplain to the British Merchants there, we do give and grant unto him our Royal licence and protection for that purpose'. The use of the term Factory was on this occasion carefully avoided, as Factories had by then been officially abolished, but the stipend paid to the Reverend Pennell of Rs. 1000$000 per annum (£220) was paid from the Contribution Fund as in the past.

In 1814 Pennell brought from London books of Common Prayer and a surplice of 'fine Irish Linen', the latter costing £5 15s. 6d. This seems an extremely high price and it is surprising that he was unable to obtain a surplice locally. No doubt the style and shape of the surplices used by the Portuguese clergy were not to his liking.

It is interesting that Pennell described himself in the Register of Marriages as 'Chaplain to the British Merchants' in the period between 1814 and 1823, a description continued by the Reverend Edward Whiteley until 1831, after which he signed the Register as 'British Chaplain'. In fact, after the termination of the Contribution Fund in 1825, the Chaplain was not directly linked to either the Merchants or the members of the British Association and Whiteley's first title for himself was not entirely correct.

Pennell resigned in 1824 and there were two candidates to succeed him, the Revd. Edward Whiteley and the Revd. Hunt. The latter was possibly a relative of Arthur Hunt, a member of the Factory and a partner in Hunt, Newman Roope & Co.

The Consul called a meeting of British Merchants on 30th June 1824, 'to take into consideration the propriety of recommending a Chaplain, vacant by the resignation of Revd. Richard Pennell'. The meeting was attended by twenty-four merchants, but seven left in protest because they were not satisfied with the manner in which it was conducted. In particular they complained that no document or testimonial was laid before the meeting in respect of one of the candidates (Whiteley). 'Without meaning at all to disparage the character and attainments of the gentlemen recommended, we assert that they are not proved'.

The Consul was also not satisfied, 'an opinion having gone abroad that the merchants have had the privilege of electing the Chaplain, I could not refrain from opposing such a pretension.'

The merchants however appear to have disregarded him and seventeen of them unanimously passed a resolution 'that the Revd. Edward Whiteley be appointed Chaplain to His Majesty's Protestant Subjects residing in this City'.

He was to be in office for forty-six years, by coincidence the same length of time as John Whitehead as Consul, and there was a certain element of fortune in the manner of both their appointments.

Whiteley was the first Consular Chaplain in Oporto, with a stipend in 1828 of £436 per annum increased by 1843 to £500. Under an Act by George IV in 1825 what were described as British Church Establishments abroad were to be maintained by voluntary subscriptions among His Majesty's subjects residing at a foreign place, but the Consul was empowered to pay for the support of the Chaplain and the maintenance of the burial grounds, to the extent of the amount which had been raised locally by subscription. The British Government was also prepared to pay half the cost of building the Church. These grants ceased in 1875, but in any case the British Chapel in Oporto had already been built a few years before this Act came into force.

The Reverend Kinsey evidently did not find a sermon from Chaplain Whiteley to his liking, when he attended service at 'The Factory Church' in 1827. He described the congregation as consisting of the most wealthy and respectable merchants in the town, the greater part of whom were English, 'but the peculiar text of the sermon at once awakened our suspicions of what the nature of the discourse was to be, when we heard it vehemently affirmed that the greater part of the congregation . . . were under the sentence of eternal reprobation and that nothing could save them'.

Kinsey was of course incorrect when he referred to the 'Factory Church', as the connection between Church and Factory, through the Contribution Fund, had ceased to exist two years earlier.

The first Consular Chaplaincies to be named under the Act of 1825 totalled 13 of which three were in Portugal at Lisbon, Oporto and Madeira. In the period 1828–51 a further 21 were added to the list.

[33]

Chapter 5

6

Resignation of Consul Crispin from British Association ☆ Early British Consuls ☆ Expected privileges by British merchants

During the first ten years after the Association was formed in 1814, the Consul presided as Chairman and signed the Minutes accordingly, and the Member in charge of the administration of the House for the year was called 'The Treasurer', an office said to have existed since 1691. However in 1824 the Consul John Crispin ceased to preside at his own request and we find the Minutes signed for the first time by the 'Treasurer & Chairman', the description used until 1845, after which it became only the 'Treasurer' – the title held ever since by the member responsible for finance and administration during his term of office of one year. Evidently the Consul took no further part in the administration of the Association once the Contribution Fund had been wound up. In fact John Crispin had been elected a Full Member in 1815, the only case on record of the Consul being a Full Member of the Association, but he resigned in 1824, no doubt due to the representations that were being made at that time to the Foreign Office by those merchants who had been denied admission to the Association and about which Crispin was later in 1830 to submit a full report. By remaining a Member he would have found it hard to be impartial, but even so his report left no doubt as to where his sympathies lay. It is interesting that Crispin had previously been Consul in Lisbon and from 1802 until 1810 was listed as a member of the Factory there.

He was clearly most unpopular with some of the merchants who submitted 'a memorial of our grievances' to the Foreign Secretary in 1825, in which they claimed that 'the lamentable division of the British Community in this place owes its origin in part, and its continuance wholly, to a line of conduct (whether collusive or supine) on the part of the Consul, which has been wholly favourable to the unjust pretentions of the Individuals with whom he formerly acted under an illegal and offensive System'.

The Consul had always been closely associated with the Factory and acted as Chairman of the Contribution Fund. There was a Consul in Oporto as long as the Factory had been in existence and probably earlier. The appointment in February 1642 by the 'King of Great Britain' (Charles I) of one Nicholas Comerforde as Consul in Oporto is recorded in the municipal archives, now preserved in the *Gabinete de Historia da Cidade*. Initially the Consuls were chosen from local merchants, in some cases during the 18th century port wine shippers, and they were selected by the Factory members themselves subject to confirmation by the Foreign Office or by the Consul-General in Lisbon. This system was still adopted as late as 1802, following the death of John Whitehead. From the minutes of a meeting held at the Factory House on 16th December 1802, the day after Whitehead's death, we learn that by the unanimous wish of the Factory William Warre was invited 'to accept the office of his late uncle as Consul'.

These minutes* only came to the knowledge of the author after the first edition of this book had been published and they contain various items of great interest which will be mentioned in later chapters. The minutes are reproduced on page 19.

A Consul was appointed in Lisbon in 1583 according to A. H. Walford (*The British Factory in Lisbon*) and Consul Hugh Lee is mentioned in the State Papers (P.R.O.) as being there in 1605. In the same records, a document in 1632 declared that 'Consuls of the English Nation had been for above one hundred years past established in the Portes of those Kingdoms to governe and assist the English merchants'.

The extent to which any Consul was able to 'governe' the merchants was doubtless very limited, as the latter were quick to complain about any interference, either real or imaginary, with their interests, whether it came from the Consul or from the local authorities.

There is no doubt that the members of the British Factories, in whichever country they were, expected and very often received considerable privileges and extra-territorial rights, and they were loud in their complaints when everything did not go as they wished. They were encouraged in this attitude by the semi-official status granted them by the authorities in London. For example, in 1741 the Admiralty instructed the Commanders of H.M. ships stationed off the Portuguese coast to obey the directions of the Oporto Factory and to be entirely at their disposal. The Factory were evidently very appreciative of the protection given by the Royal Navy and on two occasions made presentations to Naval Captains. In 1742 a silver salver was given to Captain Thomas Williams 'for his vigilant and effectual Protection on the Coast of Portugal from Spanish Privateers' and in 1762 Captain the Hon. Frederick Maitland received a handsome silver cup. The descendants of these two officers still have these presents at their homes in Somerset and Scotland. The Factory at Oporto was also very well regarded at this time by the British Minister in Lisbon, Sir Benjamin Keene, who wrote to them in 1749: 'Gentlemen, His Majesty having been pleased to order me to repair immediately to the Court of Spain, give me leave to acquaint you with the King's pleasure on this occasion and to desire you to be assured that in whatever part I may possibly be of any service to the British Factory at Porto in general or to any of its worthy members in Particular, They shall find a readiness in me to execute their Commands equal to the sincerity and warmth of my wishes for their Prosperity and Happiness. I have the Honour to be with the greatest Regard and Esteem, Gentlemen. . . .'†

In a report by a Select Committee on Consular Establishments in 1812, it was stated that 'Factories were governed by certain regulations adopted for their mutual support and assistance against the undue encroachments or interference of the Governments of the countries in which they resided'.

It is not surprising that the Portuguese government did not approve of some of the activities of the British merchants, more especially those in Lisbon, who benefited by tax exemptions and other advantages under the 1654 Treaty, but also engaged in illegal clandestine operations by the smuggling of gold coin or dust to England in both Royal Navy ships and by the regular Packet to Falmouth. Among those mentioned in 1661 was John

*Ref. P.R.O. FO 63 40 41 P 00944.
†Ref. British Library, Add: MS 32816 f.48.

Chapter 6

Page, referred to later at Viana do Castelo.

There was a considerable import of gold from Brazil in the 17th century and the first part of the 18th. Vast numbers of slaves had been shipped to Brazil from West Africa to work in the sugar and tobacco plantations and the gold and diamond mines. The imported gold was used to finance the purchase, through the British merchants, of cloth and woollen goods from England, but the export of it was prohibited. The British Envoy, Lord Tyrawley, reported to London about the clandestine dealings in gold by the English factors and how it was noticed that British naval vessels would put in to Lisbon when they had information about the arrival of ships from Brazil. 'From the indiscretion of our merchants, the Portuguese cannot be ignorant of what gold is sent out by the least attention to our conduct, since the Bills of lading to send it home, either by the Packets or Men of War, are generally signed at the Publick Coffee House and this whole transaction is publickly talked of upon the Exchange as any other matters'.

The Consuls were subject to frequent criticism both from the merchants as well as from visitors who subsequently wrote accounts of their travels. In 1787, Arthur Costigan described the Consul at Faro as 'dumb, morose and pensive'. However he was full of praise for John Whitehead who was 'versatile, sprightly and communicative in the highest degree and has a wonderful skill in adapting himself to all companies and languages he happens to meet with'. Not so favourable was the opinion of three merchants, protesting in 1830 at their exclusion from the Factory House, who complained that Consul Crispin appeared in everything to be dilatory and inattentive.*

In 1857 it was the American Consul, Nicholas Pike, who annoyed the Factory members. He had apparently replied in rude terms to an invitation to dine and it was decided that he could not henceforward be invited to the Factory House.

In 1863 what was described as an 'unpleasant affair' took place in the Factory House between George Sandeman and Consul Swift. The latter was forced to apologise which he did only verbally, but it was considered that honour was thus satisfied. The criticism may not have been all from one side, and Sellers wrote 'our ancestors in Oporto are not always described by the Consular representative in eulogistic terms'. This applied also to Lisbon in earlier days, where Consul Maynard wrote to London in 1671 'to sound Lord Arlington (the Secretary of State) on the possibility of his being allowed to sue his enemies in the English Factory at Lisbon for damages'. He added that he would send some of the choicest Oporto wines after the vintage.

The Consul had his office in the Factory House until about 1835. It is not recorded why the Consulate was moved, but possibly it was felt that the Consul was becoming too closely involved with the Factory members, as was clearly the case with Crispin. In any case, once the Contribution Fund had been abolished, the consular link with the Factory House became much less close. The situation of the Consulate prior to the building of the Factory House is not clear, and Costigan wrote that in 1787 'Consul Whitehead has no Counting House'.

At a much earlier date, there was a British Consul at Viana do Castelo. In *The Story of Two Fine Wines* (P. W. Sandeman, 1955) it is written that 'by 1578

*Ref. P.R.O. SP 63/427

the export of Portuguese wine to England from Viana do Castelo had become sufficiently important to warrant the appointment of a British Consul there'. The source for this is not given and it is to some extent in contradiction to Croft's assertion that the British wine shippers did not settle in Portugal until after the Treaty of 1654. Sellers refers to Christopher Battersby as 'Consul of the English nation at Vianna in 1700'.

Later in the 18th century, there are references in the records of Hunt Roope & Co. to payments for the 'Consul's bills at Vianna in 1790' relating to both inward and outward shipments. There are also lists of expenses incurred by their house at Viana at the same date. This firm must have been the only port shippers to have a branch office at Viana at such a late date, but it was certainly only maintained in connection with their extensive business in the import of *bacalhau* (dried cod). The 'inward' contribution for 'fish' for the year 1790 was paid in January 1791, unlike the payments to the outward Fund on wine which were normally paid at the time of shipment.

The details and dates of the early British Consular presence in Viana do Castelo and Oporto are not in themselves of paramount importance, except insofar as the Consuls were linked to a great extent with the early Factories.

A final note of interest on the subject of British Consuls is that in 1815 there was a Consul at Figueira da Foz. A payment was made to Consul Tozer there for expenses in sending off letters to the Frigate *Hyperion*.

Chapter 6

7

New lease of Factory property ☆ *Abolition of Foreign Factories in Portugal* ☆ *Re-occupation of Factory House* ☆ *Formation of British Association* ☆ *Closure and definition of Contribution Funds*

To return however to 1806, following the apparent failure to produce the Title Deeds, a new measurement and survey took place of all the ground in which the Factory House stood in order to obtain a new Lease from the Crown'.

As a result a perpetual Lease was granted on 6th December 1806 to 'William Warre, Consul of the British Nation, of the English Factory House, subject to the annual quitrent of three thousand reis'. This amount was made up of the previous rent already being paid of Rs. 2311 but apparently without any official lease, plus an additional Rs. 689 assessed as a result of the survey. It was stated by the authorities that of all this property they preserved no title deed, it having been mislaid, except that which appears from a certificate that they presented for the acknowledgement as theirs of the said property'.

It is important to note that, in accordance with a Royal Decree of 1802, Leases were only granted for the lifetime of the occupants, but in the case of the Factory House it was ruled by the Procurator of the Records that this rule could not be observed because the property was administered by an Assembly over which the Consul of the Nation presided and being thus a collective body there were no individuals qualified to appear in the Lease as Lessees for life. Therefore the Procurator ruled that the Lease be in perpetuity from this day and forever, to the Consul of the British Nation, and his Corporation and their Successors'.

One of the clauses in the Lease was to the effect that 'the said tenants and their successors shall not make over the said House, or any part of it, to any Chapel, Church, Monastery or to any holy or religious person and on no account to allow the said House to be used for the saying of Masses, Church Services, etc. under pain of the whole becoming null and void and the said tenants for any contravention shall forfeit the property to the Crown'.

This clause was certainly not complied with, because there is no doubt that Church services were held in the Ballroom of the Factory House until such time as the British Chapel was built, c. 1815–18. This is a logical deduction from the Report of the Chapel Committee of 1815, mentioned earlier, which stipulated that the Chapel should be the same size as the Factory House ballroom.

Four years later in 1810, the Factory ceased to exist as an official entity, following the Treaty between George III and the Prince Regent of Portugal, at that time in exile in Brazil. The Treaty of Amity, Commerce and Navigation was signed at Rio de Janeiro on the 19th February 1810 by the Conde de Linhares and Lord Strangford the British Minister to Lisbon. Article XXV stipulated that there should be no more British Factories in Portugal, with the following text: 'His Britannic Majesty consents to waive the Right of creating

Factories or incorporated Bodies of British Merchants under any name or description whatsoever within the Dominions of His Royal Highness the Prince Regent of Portugal . . . and His Royal Highness does also engage that he will not consent or permit that any other Nation or State shall possess Factories or incorporated bodies of Merchants within his Dominions so long as British Factories shall not be established therein'.

Strangford, an Irish Peer, had as a young man published in London a translation in verse of some of the lesser poems of Camoens and his interest in Portuguese literature may have contributed to his appointment in a junior capacity to the Legation in Lisbon, subsequently becoming Minister. He was popular in literary and social circles and in furthering British interests he was no doubt aided by the presence in Lisbon at that time of Prince Augustus, Duke of Sussex, a younger son of George III, who had gone to Portugal ostensibly for reasons of health but most likely in reality in a diplomatic role to counter the strong French influence that existed.

An interesting sequel to all this was the presentation by President Eanes of Portugal to the Queen, during his state visit to London in 1978, of a portrait of the Duke of Sussex painted in Lisbon by Domenico Pellegrini.

It was in 1811 that the members took possession of the Factory House once more, following the interruption of the French occupation. On 11th November of that year the surviving members of the old Factory resolved at a meeting that they would form a Society and that an annual Chairman be elected who should also serve the office of Treasurer. The Society continued with that title until August 1812 when the name was changed to the British Club, and this was finally altered, by a meeting held on 21st November 1814, to the British Association, which it has been called ever since.

The new title was mentioned later in a report by the Factory members to George Canning in 1824. 'In consequence of the Treaty of 1810 which stipulates that no Factories shall be established in Portugal, the Factory remaining in every other respect the same gave up this obnoxious title and assumed that of the British Club and the following year (in fact two years later) at the recommendation of Mr. Consul-General Jeffery (in Lisbon) it again altered its title, assuming that of the British Association, to avoid the word "Club".'

The story, often recounted, that a dinner or lunch was held on 11th November 1811 attended by 11 members and that this marked the actual return to the House does not appear to be confirmed by any documentary evidence and in any case it is disproved to the extent that the House had already been re-occupied by at least 4th June 1811, on which date a Ball and Supper took place. The attendance was not recorded but the cost of the entertainment, amounting to about £110, was shared by eight members and the British Doctor. The names of the former were Hinde (? Hine), Forrester, Camo, Newman, Roope, Tyndale, Burmester & Harris. These together with Messrs. Knowsley, Snow & Croft appear to have been the survivors of what was described as 'The late Factory'.

The Factory House must have been unfurnished, as chairs were hired for the occasion as well as chandeliers, dishes and knives and forks, the latter all rented from one Joseph Longstaff, who also supplied the wines. The account submitted by him was paid by the firm Webb, Campbell Gray & Camo (subsequently Taylor Fladgate & Yeatman) and shared between the eight members.

Chapter 7

Joseph Camo was an American citizen who remained in Oporto during the French occupation, except for a short period from March to June 1809.

He must have departed in haste following his letter to the firm's partners in London of the 17th March 1809 reporting that 'It is said the enemy is already advanced as far as Braga, only 8 leagues from here'. His next letter of the 9th June advised his 'safe return to this unfortunate place'.

It has often been said that Joseph Camo looked after the Factory House during the occupation, but in all his voluminous correspondence to London he never once appears to have mentioned the Factory House, at least during the critical years of 1808 and 1809, so there is no means of knowing to what extent, if any, he acted as caretaker. It also remains a mystery as to how this American became a partner in a British port wine firm, as well as the only non-British member on record of the old Factory and for a few years of the subsequent British Association.

It is interesting to note that no further mention of any British Club in Oporto appears until nearly 90 years later when an approach was made in 1902 to the British Association by a group of British residents, with the suggestion that a club be formed in conjunction with the British Association, to be based in the latter's premises in the Factory House.

The proposal was given scant consideration and after a meeting of members of the Association, attended, it should be recorded, by only eight members, and these possibly the most conservative of the shippers, it was turned down in rather peremptory terms. In fact a social club was formed in 1902 with the name of 'British Union Club', shortly changed to the 'Oporto British Club'.

In Lisbon following the abolition of their Factory the members formed the Society of Merchants and Factors in 1811 which continued in existence until the second half of the 19th century. The term 'Merchants and Factors' had been in use for a very long time and was used in the original Act of Parliament in 1721 creating the Contribution Fund.

Seemingly both in Lisbon and Oporto little attention was paid to the terms of the Treaty of 1810, under which incorporated bodies of British merchants under any name or description whatsoever were prohibited.

In July 1825 the Act of 1721 was repealed, but already the previous year the Consul had advised Members that the Contribution Fund was to be closed and the final meeting was held on 21st June 1824.

Some explanation is needed about the two Contribution Funds. The one known as the Outward Fund was a tax levied on exports to the United Kingdom in both British and Neutral vessels, and it was from this Fund, deriving mainly from the export of wine but also to a very limited extent of oil, cork and other items, that the building of the Factory House was financed.

There is no record as to when the contributions to this Fund commenced but it would appear that it started considerably after the introduction of the second 'Inward' Fund in 1721, and that it was terminated at least by 1807, if not earlier soon after the completion of the Factory House in 1790.

When the controversy arose as to the ownership of the House, the members of the British Association claimed that many of the merchants who in 1825 were demanding the right of membership had not in fact been in Oporto at the time the House was built and had not contributed to the cost.

One of the very few documents relating to events prior to the Peninsular War that survives in the Factory House is a copy of 'an extract of what had been written to Mr. Walpole*, when Ambassador at Lisbon, by the Committee of the Factory relative to sundry matters, dated 10 August 1776'. The communication read: 'The Committee answered Mr. Walpole in the terms the most respectful and sent him an Instrument signed by all the Factory (Chas. Page excepted, who absolutely refused signing) empowering the Factory to act for the general good as they thought proper and expend from the Fund raised by our Voluntary Contribution such sums as were necessary'.

This is a clear reference to the Outward Fund of which the voluntary nature was confirmed in 1824 when the Factory members wrote to George Canning, then Foreign Secretary, in connection with the ownership of the building: 'It was in 1767 that the Factory resolved to build the House which it now possesses and some of the members subscribed large sums which were to be repaid out of the proceeds of the annual voluntary contribution, this was by agreement so much per pipe on wine exported and a trifling sum on some other articles'.

The 'Inward' Fund has always received greater publicity than the 'Outward' and in fact many writers have ignored the existence of more than one Fund. The Inward Fund was a form of tax levied on all imports from Great Britain and was used to pay the Consul and British Chaplain, as well as the Doctor and the expenses of the British Hospital, and also to give assistance where needed to distressed British subjects and 'to such other pious, charitable and public uses as should be determined'. The expenses for which the Fund was responsible were very considerable, yet surprisingly Consul Crispin was of the opinion that the 'Outward' Fund very greatly surpassed the 'Inward'.

The expenses of maintaining the Factory House must have been paid from the Outward Fund from 1790 until 1807 and in the records of Hunt Roope & Co., there is a mention in 1795 of a payment to the Treasurer of the Factory Contribution on 194 pipes of wine shipped in 1794 in neutral vessels. At an earlier date, in 1781, a payment was recorded by Offley Forrester of a Contribution paid to the Factory on the export of cork.

The scale of charges payable on the exports was 300 reis per pipe on wine, 400 reis per pipe on oil and 25 reis per quintal on cork. 100 reis was the equivalent of 5d., now 2p.

*A cousin of the famous politician and writer Horace Walpole.

Chapter 7

The dispute about the ownership of the Factory House ☆ The reports of Consuls Crispin & Sorell ☆ Financing of Factory House expenses

The Report submitted in 1830 by Consul Crispin 'Relating to the Factory House at Oporto', was a sequel to the various representations that had been made to the British Government in and subsequent to 1825 by those merchants in Oporto who claimed that the Factory House was the property of the British nation and that all British subjects were entitled to use it. Crispin, in his report to His Majesty's Secretary of State, regretted the delay that had arisen 'by the endeavour to obtain thro' different channels such satisfactory information and documentary evidence as might bring this disputed Claim under one point of view for consideration and decision'.

However Crispin came to the conclusion that 'Altho the members of the Association were also Merchants in charge of the Contribution Fund, the Meetings were never blended together during the period that the Contribution Fund existed . . . and none of the monies belonging to the Contribution Fund appropriated to any purposes relating to the Factory House. . . . The Possessors have certainly from their own monies supported it since they became repossessed of the premises (i.e. in 1811)'. The Report closed with these words: 'If the Factory House were to be open for general use by Right, to all British Subjects, it could not be closed to any individual of whatever Class, male or female'.

It is interesting that one of the signatories to the 1825 Memorial, John T. Quillinan, was himself elected a member of the Association in 1834. His brother Edward, who was born in Oporto, was married to the daughter of the poet William Wordsworth. He was listed as a guest at Factory House dinners in 1845 and 1846, and he was buried in Grasmere churchyard in a grave next to Wordsworth.

Strangely, Quillinan was not a signatory to a letter addressed to the 'Gentlemen Directors of the Ball at the Factory House' dated 11th December 1824, signed by thirteen merchants who declined to attend the Ball to which they had been invited, claiming that 'the acceptance of such invitations would be inconsistent with the proceedings at present pursued by the undersigned with the view of proving that the Factory House is a Public National Property'. They also objected to the title of the British Association which 'evidently encroaches upon the rights and derogates from the respectability of the community of British merchants in this City'.

A surprising signature is that of John Graham, whose portrait painted at the age of 26, hangs in the Dining Room. But it must be remembered that at that date Graham was engaged only in the textile trade and therefore excluded from the British Association.

The representations to London continued for several years, both on the part of the Factory members and of the excluded merchants. The latter

John Graham, 1797–1886

received a rebuff to their claims in November 1831 when the Foreign Office wrote to 'Mr. L. Ormerod and others, British Merchants at Oporto. 'It is possible that the Documents which were brought to England in 1807 may contain evidence to prove that the Factory House was a national building to which all His Majesty's subjects are entitled to have access, but in the present state of the information which has been furnished to the Secretary of State, Lord Palmerston is further advised that the claim of the general body of merchants resident in Oporto to free admission into the Factory House is not made out in such a manner as will render it advisable for his Lordship to

[43]

Chapter 8

disturb the parties now in possession and who, according to the statements which have been received, have for the last eighteen years defrayed the expenses of the Establishment out of their own funds"'.

The merchants however persisted with further arguments, claiming that 'It is not a fact that the present Occupants have defrayed all the expenses of the Establishment out of their own funds, for part of the Premises has been till very lately let off in shops at rents fully adequate to keep the House in a constant state of repair'.

However the end of the affair came three years later in a sudden and rather unexpected manner, but only after Consul Sorell had returned to London on relinquishing his post. He wrote to Viscount Palmerston on 18th August 1834, 'My Lord, with reference to the different representations which have at various times since the year 1820 been addressed to the Foreign Department upon the subject of the dispute relating to the right of admission to the Building called the Factory House at Oporto, I have now the honour to lay before your Lordship extracts from two private letters I received by the last Mail from Portugal, the first from Mr. A. Cox, a respectable and intelligent Merchant and the second from Major McCrohan, a retired British Officer, both established in that City, by which it appears that these unfortunate differences have at length been brought to a close and harmony and good understanding established among the long divided British Community at Oporto'.

The letter he mentioned from Edward A. Cox was as follows: 'The promised visit of Don Pedro (the King of Portugal) is at last over, his reception was as it ought to have been most enthusiastic. Two Balls were given to him, one at the Camara, the other at the Factory. When the Members of the British Association resolved upon giving a Ball to the Royal party, they issued invitations to *all* the British Residents . . . after some discussion we agreed that our claim to the free use of the house should not be prosecuted further. Nearly all decided upon going to the Ball and when Sandeman and Forrester heard this, they advanced a step further and called upon me'.

Sorell had returned from Oporto in the brig *Camoens* after what he described as 'a tedious passage of sixteen days to Liverpool'. In contrast his successor Edwin Johnston, appointed at a salary of £500 per annum, sailed by the schooner *Pike* from Falmouth, reaching Oporto in four days, but he was unable to land due to bad weather and he was forced to continue to Lisbon, eventually arriving in Oporto in the steamer *City of Edinburgh*, seventeen days after leaving England.

Crispin may to some extent have been biased in favour of the members of the Association, but his opinion was confirmed by Consul Sorell in 1834. The latter, in a report to the Foreign Office, spoke of 'my endeavours to calm the angry feelings which have long prevailed . . . and to bring the adverse parties to a dispassionate consideration of the real merits of the case'. He continued 'The investigation has produced a material change in the opinions I had previously formed which were founded on the statements made by the gentlemen who claim admission into the House and who I believe labour under some erroneous impressions connected with the demand'.

Sorell based his decision to a great extent on the interpretation of various clauses in the lease of 1806, in particular that the Portuguese Government clearly considered the lease was granted to Consul Warre as the head of a private association and not as the agent or representative of a foreign government. Also the inclusion of the expression 'successors' precluded any possibility that the ownership belonged to the British nation (Sorell claimed that a nation has no successors) and the same applied to the British community as a whole.

At the conclusion of his long, and at times verbose report, Sorell did allow himself some slight doubts but not sufficient to change his overall verdict: 'The manner in which the building was raised may have been irregular. The rights of the possessors may be questionable, but I am at a loss to discover sufficient grounds to support a claim to the property by the British Government'.

Among the arguments put forward by the claimants were that the construction of the Factory House was under the direction of John Whitehead in his capacity as British Consul and that he 'had caused to be sculptured the British Arms which are to be seen in the vast edifice proclaiming its nationality'.

Both these points are capable of different interpretation. Whitehead did not design the building in his capacity as the British Consul, but as an architect who had already drawn the plans for other houses in the vicinity. As regards the British Arms, it is debatable whether they were displayed in the Factory House prior to Whitehead's death, because according to Consul Crispin writing in 1830, the Consular office was not there at that time, but only later when William Warre was Consul and Crispin continued it there, 'because his residence for several years was far away from the centre of trade'.

In fact the Arms were never in the room used by the Consul but, as one writer described it, 'over the entrance to the principal room (Great Saloon)'.

The Consulate was definitely in the Factory House in 1811 for a minute dated 18th November that year recorded that 'it was resolved that the Treasurer for the time being shall have the free use of the two rooms adjoining the Consul's office during his Treasureship'.

If in fact the Arms had been displayed before the war it is unlikely that they would have survived the French occupation and in that case new Arms were placed later in the Ballroom, possibly early in 1811. It was recorded that the 'Arms of the Prince Regent of Great Britain' were repainted that year and this description would date them no earlier than the beginning of 1811 when the Prince Regent (subsequently George IV) assumed that title.

Further evidence provided by the cash book of the Inward Contribution Fund for the period 1811–24 seems to reinforce still further the claim by the port shippers that they were the legitimate owners of the building. This book shows that the expenses of maintaining the Factory House were definitely not paid out of the Fund during that period.

The most conclusive evidence in the context of the membership of the Factory and the ownership of the House prior to the Peninsular War comes from the minutes of the Factory meeting on 16th December 1802, referred to earlier, as these confirm that of the 14 member houses represented at the meeting all but one can be identified as port shippers. The only exception is Pennells Follett & Co., who are not identifiable with any trade. But the Pennell family appear frequently in Oporto Church records and Richard Pennell was appointed Chaplain to the British merchants in 1814 (Page 32).

After the re-occupation of the House in 1811 a fixed annual subscription of Rs. 100$000 per member was introduced this being increased to Rs. 240$000 in 1812, the equivalent of about £53. But the system was changed in 1813,

Chapter 8

when a subscription based on exports was re-introduced payable by member firms calculated at Rs. 200 per pipe of port exported (about 10d.) plus ¼/000 on imports, 'To defray the expenses of this establishment'. The records show that in fact the tax on imports in this connection was extremely small and was in any case contributed by the port shippers.

The system of contribution remained the same until 1876 when a fixed subscription applicable to all member firms was again introduced. This was prompted no doubt by the fact that five firms, Cockburn, Croft, Offley, Sandeman and Smith Woodhouse, had resigned during the period 1863–72 in protest against the system of contribution based on shipments. As they represented a large proportion of the total membership it was clearly essential to persuade them to join again, if the Association was to be able to survive.

All did in fact re-join then with the exception of Smith Woodhouse, who returned at a later date, but even then the total membership was only 11 firms.

9

The perpetual lease ☆ Petition to reduce rateable value ☆ Purchase of freehold ☆ Ceremony of formal possession

In 1832 King Don Miguel confirmed the perpetual lease of the House with an annual rent of Rs. 3$000, but this was reduced in 1846 to Rs. 2$250 by what was described as a *Carta de Lei*. Earlier in this year the rateable value of the property had been assessed at Rs. 1000$000 (£220) by the 3rd Bairro of Cedofeita, but this was shortly after reduced to Rs. 800$000 following an appeal by the Treasurer, in which he claimed that the rent paid by other similar establishments could not be used as an analogy, especially the *Assembleia Portuense*. He minimised the activities at the Factory House as having 'only a Reading room and holding a few dinners and occasionally some other gathering, and being maintained by twenty firms'. In contrast, he claimed, at the *Assembleia Portuense* there were daily meetings, teas, various entertainments and many Balls during the year, all maintained by about 350 members.

The Balls at the Factory House and the constant entertainment held there were conveniently overlooked.

The Treasurer then sent a petition to the Queen of Portugal in which a reduction of the rateable value to Rs. 500$000 was requested on the grounds that other buildings in Oporto of 'equal grandeur and magnificence' were assessed on a lower scale and documents were submitted to support this claim. The Treasurer also quoted Article 1 of the Treaty of 29th July 1842 under which British subjects had the same civil rights as the Portuguese and were obliged to pay on the same scale 'neither more favoured nor too highly assessed'. The appeal achieved no result and was turned down by the Oporto tax authorities on 11th March 1847.

Whereas in the 18th century and earlier it was nothing unusual for the members of the British Factory to complain to the highest authority when everything did not go as they wished, it seems remarkable that as late as 1846 they should petition direct to the Queen on a matter of such comparatively little importance. On the other hand, in the time of John Whitehead it would not have been necessary, such was his influence with the local authorities, although even he could not obtain permission to build a British church, which doubtless he would have wished to do at the same time as he bought the land for the cemetery in 1785, up to that time forbidden.

However the question of the rateable value of the Factory House property was overtaken by an event of very considerable importance. Under a Royal Decree of 29th December 1846, it became possible to terminate the leasehold and purchase the freehold of the property. This appears to have been a general decree applying to all leasehold property and there is no evidence that it was a favour or a privilege granted exclusively to the British Association, as has frequently been stated.

Strangely enough the Association did not take advantage of this opportunity until two years later, when the Treasurer, John Alexander Fladgate, paid on the 27th December 1848, to the *Cofres Centraes* of the District of Oporto the sum of Rs. 35$100. The actual amount due was Rs. 31$500, but according to the receipt, in the possession of the Association, there was a surcharge payable because some of the money was paid in notes and not in coin.

The sum paid, the equivalent of only about £8, seems ridiculously low, especially in relation to the rateable value of the property which had been fixed at about £180, but possibly one reason was that as freehold owners of the property the Association would in future pay the property tax, equivalent of rates, which would certainly be higher than what they had paid previously as tenants. In fact in 1850 the tax paid was about 50 per cent higher than previously, and by 1860 it was first described as *Contribuição Predial*, the term used today.

The date on which the Association became the legal owner of the property is not clearly established because, although the purchase price of the freehold was paid in December 1848, it was not until two years later on 26th December 1850 that a Royal Decree recapitulated all that had transpired and confirmed that the Association 'from now onwards owned and enjoyed the said property free of any liability on it and with exemption from the aforesaid charge'. This last clause was a reference to the annual leasehold rent that had previously been paid. It was also stipulated that no property transfer tax was to be paid on the transaction.

A further six months elapsed before a ceremony traditional in Oporto at that time took place at the Factory House on 16th June 1851 at which the Treasurer, John Ramsay Thomson, took formal possession of the freehold, 'opening and closing doors and windows and declaring in a loud and intelligible voice the ownership of the property'. It was recorded that 'there was no contradiction by any person'. A certificate was issued the following day by the *Repartição da Fazenda do 3° Bairro* in Oporto to the effect that twenty-four hours had passed and no opposition had been lodged by anyone

It is surprising that there was no mention of this ceremony in the minutes of any members' meetings during 1851, nor had the purchase of the freehold been recorded during the period 1848 to 1850, except for the entry of the payment in the cash book. The reason for this may not be hard to find. At the time, the change of ownership of the property from a perpetual lease to freehold may not have seemed of any great importance to the members. In either case their tenure of the House would have seemed to them equally secure; and events that will prove of great interest, historically and socially, to subsequent generations are taken very much for granted at the time they occur. Not only did the members apparently fail to record this important event, but also they showed little concern for the documents connected with it.

Only in 1898, about fifty years later, was the Consul, Mr. Honorius Grant, asked by the members to verify that the title deeds of the House were in order. Following his assurance that they were, it was decided that 'the documents belonging to the British Association be placed in the safe of the London & Brazilian Bank and that copies of such documents as may be considered of sufficient importance be made by a Notary Public and kept in the Factory House'.

At the next meeting, early in 1899, they decided that the only document of sufficient importance was that described as the *remissão do forro* on the premises, the equivalent of the freehold title, and a copy of this 'was made and deposited in the box of the British Association'. There is no record as to whether in fact any documents were ever deposited at the bank.

But whatever the reaction of the members at the time there is no doubt that the acquisition of the outright ownership of the House was of great importance and constituted a landmark in the history of the Factory House. It also coincided with the ending of a long period of uncertainty during which the tenure of the property was perhaps considered of less importance than the internal disputes which certainly divided the British community.

Archibald Cockburn (d. 1892)

Chapter 9

10

Formation of Pombal's Wine Company ☆ Influence of John Whitehead on Oporto architecture ☆ Description of the Factory House and the principal rooms

For an appreciation of the contents of the Factory House and of the character and style of the principal rooms in it, some explanation is useful of the circumstances that contributed to the radical change in architectural fashion in Oporto during the second half of the 18th century.

An indirect cause of this change may be traced to the founding in 1756 of the *Companhia Geral da Agricultura das Vinhas do Alto Douro* by the Marquis of Pombal, the 'Dictator' Minister of King D. José I. The declared intention behind the formation of the Company was to safeguard the interest of the Douro farmers, to establish fair prices and at the same time to create a demarcated area in which the Factory wines, that is those destined for shipment to England, were to be produced.

Whereas the principal objectives were to harm the British shippers and to attempt to break their monopoly of the finest wines in the Douro district, there can be little doubt that the Factory, if not actually providing the pretext for the establishment of the Company, were instrumental in hastening its formation by their high-handed behaviour towards the Douro farmers, whom they accused of adulterating their wines, that is by the addition of elderberry juice (*baga*) to give more colour, a practice not by any means confined to the 18th century but subject then to severe penalties including imprisonment. The shippers threatened to punish the worst offenders by refusing to buy their wines again. In 1755 the demand for wine was very low and the Factory made few purchases even though the growers offered their wines at extremely low prices. They sent a delegation to Oporto to plead with the shippers, but to no avail, and then sent representatives to Lisbon to present their grievances, producing a letter which the Factory had unwisely written in strong terms for distribution through their Commissaries in the wine district.

This situation gave Pombal all the excuse he needed and his Company was formed in 1756. Then it was the turn of the Factory to protest at what they described as the infringements of their privileges under the Treaties. Pombal in return declared that he had never heard of any British Factory except one 'on the coast of Coromandell'. This is a reference to the east coast of India where the British had founded factories at Madras and other centres in the seventeenth century. Pombal also considered it was very insolent of the English to give themselves such consequence by printing so dictatorial a letter over the name of the English Factory.

James Murphy had a strange theory about Pombal and the Company, which can hardly be taken seriously. Murphy had been much impressed by the politeness of the customs officials on his arrival at Oporto. 'Those who have witnessed the visits of British custom house officers upon similar occasions will scarcely believe that so much urbanity exists among men of that

Entrance Hall or Piazza of Factory House

class. The late Marquis de Pombal on his arrival as Ambassador to the British Court was so rudely treated by a group of these gentry that it impressed him ever after with an unfavourable idea of the execution of the revenue laws of this country and it is generally supposed that this circumstance alone operated as the cause of the regulations which he afterwards established relative to the wine trade of Oporto, regulations not very friendly to the interests of the British Factory of that city. But the opposition to the Company continued and in 1757 Pombal sent his cousin, João de Almada, to be Governor of Oporto with a special mission to try and calm the situation and to subdue the opponents of the Company.

It happened that Almada was also acting as chairman of the Oporto public works department and in this capacity was interested in plans for transforming the area round the Praça da Ribeira, facing the River Douro, and in the new street of São João. In view of Almada's connection with Pombal it is remarkable that he should have become such an intimate friend of Consul John Whitehead, as certainly seems to have been the case, for the latter was

[51]

so closely linked with the Factory who were the bitterest opponents of Pombal's *Companhia*.

In 1763 plans were submitted to the King for enlarging the old Praça da Ribeira as part of these extensive schemes of urban development. The scale of the new square, which was never completed, would have resembled the imposing Praça do Comercio (the former Terreiro do Paço) on the waterfront in Lisbon, built in the Pombaline style. It is certain that Whitehead's influence, and his involvement in these projects, led the Governor to adopt a Neo-classical style inspired by Palladian architecture and completely opposed to the Baroque architecture current until then in Oporto.

Whitehead has been described as an amateur architect, but this description does not do him justice, and it is obvious that he must have had some training and studied architecture prior to coming to Portugal. He designed the elevations for the west side of the projected Praça da Ribeira, which were approved by Almada, as well as making plans, dated 1774, for a large new square at the top of the Rua S. João, by the lower end of the Rua das Flores. These designs have survived and are preserved in the *Gabinete da Historia*, Oporto. Only the west side of the square was in fact finished in accordance with Whitehead's plans, but some of the houses there have since been considerably altered by the addition of extra storeys, as also was the case with houses near the Factory House, and the balance and harmony of the original concept has thus been spoilt.

A design for the facade of the Factory House was discovered in the building in 1984, hidden under a staircase and in very bad condition. After lengthy restoration it is now on display in the Museum, and although not signed or dated it would appear to be without doubt the work of John Whitehead. A significant similarity between this plan and those mentioned above is that the scale in each case is also given in polegadas (inches), which differed from the normal practice of mentioning only palmos (about 9 inches).

The Palladian style of building had first been introduced into England by Inigo Jones early in the 17th century and was subsequently revived by Lord Burlington about a century later. By the time John Whitehead came to Oporto in 1756 the fashion in architecture in England was changing again towards a revival of the early classical styles from Greece and Rome, and it is surprising that he should have been in Oporto for nearly thirty years before designing the Factory House in a style that had ceased to be popular abroad, although he was able to convince the local authorities that it was still suitable for Oporto at that period. Whereas earlier in the 18th century it was not unusual for 'amateur' architects to influence building tastes, often on a theoretical level, it certainly seems that Whitehead was able to do more than that and to become to a great extent professionally involved in the execution of his designs, which may have been influenced by Carr's grandiose plans for the Hospital. In Coimbra a similar example can be found in William Elsden who was Director of Public Works at the University in the 1770s and responsible for the design of several buildings there. He served in the Portuguese Army as Engineer Colonel, but there is no evidence that he had any professional connection with Whitehead or with any civil architecture in Oporto. There is no doubt that there was considerable British influence in town planning in Oporto at that time. The growth of the city in the second half of the 18th century was very rapid. This was attributed to the great expansion in foreign trade through Oporto and to the fact that many families

The Factory House at Oporto

View of the Staircase from the Entrance Hall

had come to live in the north of Portugal following the Lisbon earthquake in 1755. One writer considered this and 'the number and degree of culture of the British community connected with the Port wine trade' to have influenced the city architecture and subsidiary decorative arts of that period in Oporto.

In the same vein, Richard Croker, writing about his visit to Oporto in 1780, considered that 'The example and encouragement of the British Factory have been attended with singularly good effects. The appearance of the country and the manners of the inhabitants in the vicinity of Oporto improve daily'.

As regards the Factory House building itself, the simple lines of the front of the house, and the sombre granite in which it is built, combine to give it a distinctly plain appearance, which is in marked contrast to the elegance of the principal rooms.

There are however a few details which relieve the monotony of the front. The central section, comprising the three centre windows, is slightly advanced and the pediments are triangular, and not segmental as those above the other windows. Also the balustrade above the main front is interrupted by the introduction of an attic which is adorned with three swags of fruit. Murphy said that it was Whitehead's intention to crown it all with a statue

[53]

Chapter 10

General view of the Ballroom, showing Vieira painting through door at rear

and that he had filled two pages of a folio book with algebraic calculations to prove how much a figure ought to recline back, so as to appear perfectly upright to a spectator standing at right angles with the front of the building at any required distance.

He added, 'what figure this will be is not yet determined, though every man of the Company has given his opinion on the subject. I suppose the wiseheads will have it of a piece with the rest of the building. A figure of Commerce, pouring grapes out of a cornucopia, the head decorated with vine leaves etc., I think would be in character with the intention of the building'.

Murphy was full of suggestions and in another passage he mentioned that the Factory had not yet decided about the statue and 'in all probability would not for some time, as artists are generally the last who are consulted on these occasions. We should suppose that in a commercial edifice like this taking the country into consideration, a statue of Prince Henry, the Pharaoh of navigation and the source of commerce, would not be unsuitable'.

Murphy, who was a distinguished artist, was plainly rather hurt that he had evidently not been consulted, but Prince Henry was to have his statue

The Factory House at Oporto

about a hundred years later, not on the top of the Factory House but in the new square that was opened up not far from it on the west side, when the name of the street was changed to Rua Infante D. Henrique.

The difficult decision over the statue, with the members all giving different advice, proved too much even for Whitehead and so the building remained without a statue.

On the ground floor is a loggia about 80 feet in length, in Palladian style, with seven arched openings and this leads into the entrance hall, or Piazza, divided into three aisles with Tuscan pilasters and six columns supporting shallow vaults.

The Hall, which some writers called the Exchange, was used as a parking place for the sedan chairs and the benches at the sides were for the bearers. In 1939 during repairs in the Hall, several apertures were found in the walls and three bottles of Vintage Port were deposited in them with a record written on vellum.

Immediately to the right on entering the Hall was the newsroom, to which visitors were admitted and the ships' captains met there to gather the latest news.

The Hall leads to the central newel staircase which is constructed round an open well. Each step is from a single piece of granite and the landings are embedded in the wall. The wrought iron balustrade was made locally, in the same style as the exterior balconies on the principal floor. This was a new fashion in England at that time, introduced from Italy, although wrought iron work had been made in Oporto for several centuries and can be seen on old houses in several parts of the city, notably in the Rua das Flores and Rua das Taipas and in altar screens dating from the 16th century in the Cathedral and other churches. Another example of this wrought iron work in the Factory House is to be found in the Ballroom Gallery. Here the style is the same but the pattern different from that of the staircase and balconies.

The central room on the mezzanine floor is low with a vaulted ceiling and leads on the west side to a room of similar proportions used as a writing room. On the other side, across a corridor running through to the kitchen situated below the Dining Room, is the Library which occupies most of the side of the building facing Rua S. João and has seven windows.

The staircase continues to the landing outside the principal rooms on the main floor. In the centre is the Ballroom, a large well-proportioned room measuring 55 feet by 29 feet 6 inches, with Ionic pilasters crowned by a full entablature with a coved ceiling above the cornice. The decoration of the panels is in a style resembling that of Robert Adam. There are three large windows with three smaller ones above them corresponding to the upper storey. The Ballroom has seven chandeliers, the largest being of thirty lights, and at the end opposite the windows, above the main door, is a musicians' gallery with three arched alcoves corresponding to the upper windows facing the street. The gallery is reached by a small staircase leading from the landing outside the Drawing Room. The redecoration of the Ballroom is a costly undertaking, only carried out at lengthy intervals. It was recorded that it was done in 1868 at a cost equivalent to £300. In more recent times it was done in 1960 and 1982, in the latter year the cost being the equivalent of £2,700.

Behind the gallery a door leads to the old Kitchen, which is lit by a skylight in the same manner as the main staircase. This kitchen lies directly above the Dining Room which was reached by a narrow circular staircase. The Billiard

Chapter 10

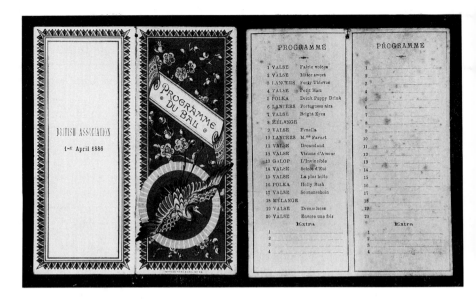

Room is directly above the Dessert Room.

Parallel to the Ballroom are the Drawing Room and the Dessert Room. The former has two doors, one from the main landing, the other from the Ballroom, and two long windows facing the front of the House. It is a long narrow room with simple decoration, two chandeliers and three built-in vitrines for the display of china.

The Dessert Room opens out of the Ballroom and also has two doors leading from the Dining Room. There are two windows facing the front and three at the side, but two further windows on the east side were at one time blocked, although the balconies remain. There are three chandeliers.

The Dining Room is entered by a door from the main landing and has four windows facing the east side. These however are not of the same height as those in the Dessert Room and their balconies are not in alignment with the others on that side of the House. This was necessary to compensate for the steep fall in the level of the street. The Dining Room has two vitrines for china and the overmantel, in the Adam style, is similar to that in the Dessert Room.

It is interesting to note that the three reception rooms on the main floor, apart from the Ballroom which is obviously the largest room in the House, are all of different dimensions, the Drawing Room being longer but slightly narrower than the Dining and Dessert Rooms, and the latter the same width but a little longer than the Dining Room.

11 Furniture, Chandeliers and China

No records survive covering the period between the building of the Factory House, completed in 1790, and the time when the members were forced, in 1807, to abandon it during the Peninsular War. This means that there is no possibility of knowing how the Factory House was furnished in the early days nor what were the contents.

However, from a study of the accounts for the years following the re-occupation of the House in 1811, it is evident that either it was extremely sparsely furnished from the beginning or else most of the contents must have been pillaged during the French occupation of Oporto. This can be stated with some certainty, because not only were items of furniture on loan or hire in 1811 and for many years after, but also glass and crockery. There are constant references to the hire of these items and curtains were hired until 1832 and chandeliers as late as the 1860s.

The first items to be bought were tables and chairs, but initially in very small quantities.

The early purchases are however notable for the fact that some of the chairs were made by a cabinet maker of considerable renown in Portugal at that time. This was José Francisco de Paiva, who was born in Oporto in 1744, and was responsible for the designs, not only of furniture and interior decorations and fireplaces, but also for churches and public buildings in the north of Portugal. Many of these designs have survived and are preserved in the *Museu Nacional de Arte Antiga* in Lisbon. A comprehensive study of his work was published in Lisbon in 1973 by Maria Helena Mendes Pinto in which some of the designs are reproduced. These show the style of Robert Adam which Paiva imitated and his furniture followed the designs of Chippendale, Sheraton and Hepplewhite. In his later period, after the end of the 18th century, he tended to concentrate more on the architectural side of his work. It is possible that he had made some furniture for the Factory House at the time it was built, because he worked with the architect Teodoro Maldonado and the latter was a close collaborator of John Whitehead, but whatever furniture might have been in the House had disappeared at the end of the occupation of Oporto by the French.

The first account from Paiva is dated 7th April 1814 and refers to 12 chairs supplied at a cost of Rs. 4$800 each, the equivalent of about 12s. He described the chairs as being made of a wood named *d'olio*, a reference to an African mahogany type, Adina Sp., used by cabinet makers of that period and mentioned by Paiva in his design for a piece of furniture illustrated in the work by Maria Mendes Pinto. The chairs can be identified with a set in the Factory House with backs in the wheatsheaf design, a style popular in England in the second half of the 18th century and of which there are several

The Dessert Room

examples in private ownership in Oporto. Originally upholstered in red velvet, they were subsequently re-covered, and again in 1987, and are now in the Map Room and on the landing of the principal floor. Two chairs in the same style but with different designs for the backs were apparently by a different maker, as are six chairs with arms, in the same design as those made by Paiva, and these were bought in 1845 from one António Pinto who in the same year repaired the original Paiva chairs.

Then in August 1815, Paiva supplied 24 chairs for the 'Factoria' at the same price. No description was given on his account, but they must have been cane-seated mahogany chairs, of which there are a total of about 150 in the House. The greater part of these are in the rope-back Regency style, the remainder being of the plainer ladder-back type.

Further similar chairs were purchased later, 25 in 1816, 60 in 1819 and a final 36 from António Pinto in 1845, these being ordered 'for the dessert room'. Some of the cane seated chairs were at first used in the Ballroom, the inventory of 1838 listing 53 chairs in that room and 36 in the Dining Room. The chairs were mostly withdrawn from the Ballroom in 1847 when mahogany benches and sofas were purchased. Either one or both have been used since and a photograph taken at the end of the 19th century shows the benches against the walls and the sofas in front of them. Then for a long

The Factory House at Oporto

period only the sofas were used, but in 1982 the benches were replaced alone, thus displaying the lower part of the wall panels to better advantage.

Many of the works of José Francisco de Paiva were signed and dated by him but regrettably no marks are to be found on any of the chairs that he made for the Factory House. He was known to have several clients among the members of the port wine trade, notably Joaquim Kopke, Isaac Mitchell of Warre & Co. and John Searle of the firm Stephenson & Searle. For the latter Paiva designed a set of chairs and a settee.

The fireplace mantels in the Dining and Dessert Rooms at the Factory House are similar in style to those of Paiva, which were taken from late 18th century neo-classical English designs, showing the influence of the Adam brothers.

It would be satisfactory to be able to attribute to José Francisco de Paiva the set of chairs in the Drawing Room that have always been the subject of controversy. These have frequently been attributed by writers, without any documentary evidence at all, to Chippendale. The latter died in 1779 before the Factory House was completed and the opinion of experts who have examined the chairs is unanimous and to the effect that they are most certainly not original or genuine Chippendale, nor indeed very perfect reproductions from his designs. They are considered to be too heavy and lacking in delicacy, although admittedly they could have been copied, not very faithfully, at a later date by a local cabinet maker, from Chippendale's design books, which were known to have been used in Portugal. Their style was very popular in Oporto in the latter part of the 18th century, described as D. José I, and Maria Helena Mendes Pinto refers to the existence of chairs of this type in the British Factory House similar to those designed by José Francisco de Paiva, but the evidence clearly shows that they were not made by him.

The chairs in question can without any doubt be attributed to a cabinet maker in Oporto, António José Correia. His account dated 11th April 1835 mentions 12 chairs with arms and two without, made in *pau preto*, a Brazilian hardwood, with seats and backs in leather. They cost the equivalent of £1 10s. each. As there is no other set of 12 armchairs in the House this evidence would appear to be conclusive. The chairs were described in the cash book as being 'For the Reading Room' and this tallies with the inventory for that room in 1838.

In 1845 it was evidently considered that the Drawing Room needed additional and more elegant furnishings, as well as re-decoration and that the chairs would be more suitable for that room than for the Reading Room. A settee was bought in mahogany with 'spring upholstered seat, horsehair bolsters and silk tassels and cording'. It was re-covered in 1987 and is now in the Map Room.

In 1848, the chairs were covered with scarlet silk damask, 14 pieces of paper hangings in a blue and white pattern were brought from England and a triple chair-back settee, matching the chairs, was bought secondhand in Lisbon.

The only possible link, albeit remote, between Chippendale and the Factory House is through John Carr. The latter designed Harewood House in Yorkshire and Chippendale, who was born in Otley not far from York, was commissioned to make several other items of furniture for Harewood in the 1770s. He would have been well known to Carr and no doubt John Whitehead was acquainted with his designs, but this certainly does not establish any direct connection with the Factory House chairs, whose provenance is the work

Chapter 11

of a local cabinet maker, based possibly on Chippendale's 'Gentleman & Cabinet Maker's Director' first published in 1754.

In the Dining Room are 30 mahogany chairs with upholstered seats and backs in green leather. They have always been in the same room since they were made locally, in 1851, by a cabinet maker, João António Vianna, at a cost of about £1 15s. 0d. each. The existence of the original account definitely disproved the opinion of some experts who believed that these chairs were brought from England, as their style is very similar to the 'Club' chairs popular there at that period. They were most certainly copied from English designs. The same maker supplied three sideboards in 1854 of a Brazilian wood 'Vinhatico'; these are in the Dining Room. The Treasurer for that year, John Fladgate, described them as 'Canterbeiries'.

Two interesting and attractive pieces of furniture are the ottomans. One of them is of four seats so placed that the occupants face different ways. The other is a circular continuous settee, with a padded pillar in the centre. Both are of the Victorian period and there is a record of the purchase in 1879 of one ottoman, but unfortunately, as was so often the case, the member firm who imported, or bought locally, the item in question did not supply the original invoice and therefore identification is not possible. In some cases an account for import duties proves that the items were imported, as in 1879 with three chairs bought from John Howard & Sons of 25 Berners Street, London W. One was described as an Easy Chair in canvas, with rosewood legs and covered in Morocco; the second also with rosewood legs in Morocco, and the third 'with shaped legs in Morocco'. All these are hard to identify. In fact these chairs if they still exist are the only ones in the building which can definitely be said to have come from England.

It is difficult to establish when the various tables in the House were bought. Where accounts exist, they are lacking in detail and identification is seldom possible. The first purchase was in 1815 when a 'Horse Shoe table' was bought from José dos Santos for about £9. Whether this was one of the end tables, for use in either the Dining or Dessert Rooms is not clear, but the tables now in these rooms must have been bought at an early date, as from accounts of dinners at least by 1827 both rooms were sufficiently furnished for the guests to move to the Dessert Room for the dessert and port.

The 1838 inventory lists '5 tables and 2 end tables in each room, forming one large table' and there is no doubt at all that all these tables, in mahogany, were made locally.

The custom of moving to the Dessert Room after dinner was probably in force from the earliest days of the Factory House, and is of course still observed today. In 1827 Kinsey, writing of a dinner he had attended given in honour of General Sir Thomas Stubbs, said: 'We have lately had the pleasure of dining with the members of the Factory at their elegant house in the Rua Nova dos Inglezes. The ballroom is the exact size of the Factory Chapel and certainly is a very fine apartment. Our dinner was superb and we adjourned from the table to another room, en suite with the first, where such a dessert and such wines were served up, as quite to astonish our northern experience'.

Possibly the custom originated from the Oxford and Cambridge colleges, but at these the same place at table is not necessarily taken by each diner when adjourning to the second room − indeed the reverse is the case − whereas at the Factory House it has usually been the practice to keep the same table seating in each room.

[60]

There are references to card tables in 1811 and repairs to the billiard table in 1812 which gives an indication of the type of pastimes that were popular. Clearly the billiard table was too difficult to remove at the time of the French occupation. Evidently the players did not treat the billiard table too well as repairs to the cloth were frequent in subsequent years, and a new table was bought in 1863 from Thurston and Co., London, at a cost of 55 guineas.

The table in the Drawing Room, at which the Treasurer presides at meetings of members, was made locally in 1845 and was described as a 'large round table in *vinhatico* wood (a Brazilian hardwood) with mahogany veneer with four columns'. The cost was the equivalent of £7. Two card tables in the same style were made the same year. One is on the landing outside the Ballroom, and the other just outside the Dining Room; also a mahogany footstool, which does not appear to have survived.

The lighting in the principal rooms was by means of candles and chandeliers, which were hired until after the middle of the century. It was not until 1842 that there was any thought of buying chandeliers. In that year the Committee appointed 'to examine the Furniture belonging to the British Association' reported that, in order to avoid the necessity and expense of hiring chandeliers and other articles on the occasion of Balls and parties, they recommended that the Ballroom should have three chandeliers, one of 48 lights and two of 30 lights, making a total of 108 lights. However nothing was done to implement that decision for several years and the first chandelier to be bought was in 1845, described as being of 16 lights, but this was hung, not in the Ballroom, but in the Drawing Room, at the end overlooking the street.

Then in 1849, three more were bought from Sedgwick & Taylor, 'Lamp & Lustre Manufacturers, of 186 Piccadilly, opposite the Albany'. They cost £88 5s. 9d. and were shipped by the S.S. *Edgar* from London and the original documents survive. These chandeliers have always been in the Dessert Room, two being of 12 lights and one of 18.

At a meeting of the members in January 1848 it was voted to purchase chandeliers for the Ballroom but the decision was reversed at a subsequent meeting, and it was not until 1851 that any action was taken to provide permanent lighting in the Ballroom, when two chandeliers came from London, costing £109. These were supplemented by two more of 12 lights each in 1858. At the same period brass 'half-circles' were bought in London, of which two were of four lights each, from Sedgwick & Dawson Ltd. in 1858, two each of eight lights in 1860 'for the Ball Room' and two in the same year of six lights 'for the Reading Room'.

All these light brackets are now in the Drawing Room. A further two chandeliers were bought in 1883 of 12 lights each, and the total number shown in the 1885 inventory was 12, the same as exist today.

It appears that no crystal chandeliers were ever considered for the Dining Room. In 1854 the accounts refer to refurnishing the room and the purchase of three light brackets. The 1838 inventory had mentioned a large metal chandelier in the Dining Room and this was evidently in use, lit with candles and subsequently possibly with gas for a considerable time until electric wall brackets were installed.

However all this lighting was evidently considered not sufficient for the grand occasions and at the 1863 Ball in honour of the King various light fittings and 24 chandeliers and paraffin lamps, together with a large amount of gas piping, was supplied for hire by William Mitchell, of 82 Rua dos Inglezes.

Chapter 11

Candles were an expensive item and were regularly imported from England, described as 'Sperm Candles'. Their use continued after the introduction of gas in 1860, and in 1869 an import was recorded of 200 lbs. 'Prize Medal Paraffine Candles, Patent Ends' from Barclay Son & Co. late Field & Co., of 34 Wigmore Street, Cavendish Square, 'Oil Merchants to Her Majesty', at a total cost of £15 8s. 10d. Presumably the wax candles available locally, and used in the churches, burnt too quickly and were not suitable for use in the chandeliers, whereas the imported candles lasted much longer.

In some parts of the House oil lamps were used, and also one outside the House in 1816 for 'the corner' and frequent accounts were paid for oil for this lamp and expenses for lighting and repairing it.

Electricity was first introduced in 1919 and the following year it was connected to the chandeliers in the Drawing Room. It was not until 1965 that the Ballroom chandeliers were wired for electricity.

Many rooms were heated with coal fires, the coal being imported 'by the pipe', often from Newcastle. There are many references to the Fire Engine; for example in 1836, 'Engine keeper, Expences with five fires', and earlier, 'Repairs to the fire engines'. The meaning is not clear. Possibly it was some form of machine for cleaning the chimneys. For very many years, the Factory House employed their own fireman, and in a letter undated one José Francisco Moreira described himself as Master Fireman and asked to retire after 40 years service and for his son to be appointed in his place. The letter was addressed to the Treasurer, George Knowsley, and like many other letters and accounts in the early days the Spanish (or perhaps Latin) *Factoria* was used instead of *Feitoria*. Evidently the fire engine was considered very efficient as in 1832 the Oporto Town Council asked if they could borrow it if the pumps in the City proved insufficient to deal promptly with any fire. The Treasurer agreed to their request. In contrast, it was recorded in 1942 that Members considered that the House was entirely devoid of means of putting out a fire. The only comment made was that it was the duty of Fire Brigades to put out fires.

The first fire insurance policy was taken out with the Phoenix Insurance Company in January 1825 for an insured value on the building and on furniture, plate, glass and wine in bottle of Rs. 20,000$000 (£4,400). The original Policy has survived and is framed in the Map Room.

There was a claim on this Policy in 1857 for a fire that 'broke out in the chimney of a room on the ground floor occupied by a servant who constantly burns a stove therein. It is supposed to have been caused by an undue accumulation of soot in the chimney which was swept about four months ago'. The fire could not have caused great damage as the claim only amounted to about £6. The room may have been on the left of the entrance hall, and the fireplace there is still in use.

In describing the most important contents of the House, the china is perhaps the easiest to identify with any certainty, although surprisingly in previous writings on the subjects the authors have invariably ascribed incorrect dates to several of the services.

In 1813 a list of purchases of china and glass and kitchen utensils was authorised, but these did not arrive from England until June 1818. The list included a Spode tea and coffee service of 24 tea cups and 24 coffee cups, with respective saucers, a teapot, bowl, milk jug and sugar bowl. Until this date, there had been frequent references to the hire and loan of tea cups, and in

1813 tea urns were purchased and three dozen silver teaspoons. Part of the Spode service, in white with floral design, has survived and is on display in the Drawing Room. The teapot is in remarkably fine condition and appears little used and possibly this was the case because tea must have been served from the urns. The marking on this service shows the word *SPODE*, with the number 2527, some in gold lettering and some in red.

With the same shipment in 1818 came a quantity of plates etc. for the dining room, including four dozen soup plates, nine dozen side plates and five dozen small plates, as well as soup tureens, vegetable dishes, casseroles with lids, salad bowls and 21 large dishes. Only one plate appears to have survived from this service. It is white with a green border and marked *Sharpus & Co Cockspur Street*. In the 1818 London Directory (Guildhall Library) there is a firm of this name listed, and also an Edward Sharpus at the same address, described as a 'China & Glass manufacturer and Staffordshire warehouse'. At this period there were numerous small china manufacturers and retailers in London, many in the St. Paul's area, and several of the Sharpus family were engaged in this trade. In 1818 R. Sharpus & Co. was listed at 33 Berkeley Square and, in 1836, Thos. and Frederick Sharpus at the same 13 Cockspur Street.

With the same 1818 shipment came a dessert service, also Spode, consisting of 42 plates and some dishes and these were described in subsequent inventories as the 'Old dessert service, white with flowers'. In 1831 a further 24 dessert plates came from London described as 'Spodes, to match the Dessert Plates at the Factory House, at 4s. 6d. each'. Of the original dessert service, many pieces have survived, including ten of the plates and some dishes in various shapes and sizes, all in very good condition. The service is marked *SPODE*, in red with the number 2248.

The four surviving plates from those that came in 1831 have no marks or numbers. All these are displayed in the Drawing Room.

The Spode tea service is of opaque porcelain which was sold with great success on the Continent during that period, the first quarter of the 19th century. It is light in weight and with a very smooth glaze.

In May 1836 it was resolved that 'Complete sets, say a dinner service, dessert service, glass and some small waiter be ordered from England'.

The dinner service was described as 'A fine Porcelain dinner service, rich broad green band, gold lines and painted flowers in centre No. 5718'. The maker was Copeland Garrett and the description *Felspar Porcelain, late Spode*. This mark was used by the factory at Stoke-on-Trent during the period 1833–47. The firm was the successor to the Spode factory, being a partnership between William Taylor Copeland, a former partner of the Spodes, and Thomas Garrett a salesman of the firm. Previously three generations of the Spode family had managed the firm under their own name.

The dinner service arrived in Oporto in 1836 and comprised 150 large plates at 3s. 3d. each, 50 soup plates at the same price and 100 smaller plates at 2s. 6d. The total cost amounted to £87 12s. 0d. Much of this service still survives and is used at both luncheons and dinners. In recent times a new service was made in Portugal by the Vista Alegre factory, to imitate the original service, but the colours are not perfectly reproduced.

By the same ship in 1836 came the dessert service, considered the most beautiful of the Factory House china, which has been greatly admired by many visitors. The service comprised 80 plates costing 7s. each, 32

Items from early Spode tea and dessert services

compotiers, eight each in square, shell, oval and round shapes, four sweetmeat stands, four cream tureens and stands and two centre pieces, for a total cost of £74 1s. 0d. Much has survived and is still in regular use. In the records the service was described as 'Maroon ground richly painted with Flowers in compartments traced with Gold', but the maker's name was not mentioned, and as the china is unmarked identification has not been possible. The service was always attributed to Coalport, but this has now been disproved not only by the Coalport Company themselves but by other expert sources, including the Victoria & Albert Museum. Whilst they are unanimous that the service was made by a Staffordshire factory, it has not been possible to identify the maker. Among those suggested has been John Ridgway of Hanley, who specialised in dessert services during the period 1830–55. But this possibility has been discounted by Coalport's, who hold many of the Ridgway pattern books, and by Geoffrey Godden, the acknowledged expert on Ridgway, who is also of the opinion that the service was not made by either Coalport or Minton or by any of the larger English firms. He suggests, but without conviction, that the maker might have been Davenport or Daniel.

The next service of importance to be brought from England was a Davenport tea service that arrived in March 1842 and is included in the 1846 inventory, listing 13 dozen cups and saucers. The invoice shows that there were also '13 cream ewers and 13 sugar boxes' and the shipment was by the brig *Anne* from London at a cost, including freight and insurance, amounting to £41 5s. 0d. The premium paid for the insurance was two per cent. Each cup and saucer cost 3s. 8d. Strangely the custom house entry and account for duties were only completed in 1845 and the duties were calculated at 16$000 per *arroba* (15 kilos) for a total of 60 kilos, equivalent in all to £17.

The Factory House at Oporto

The service was described as 'Salmon ground, Flowers and Gilt'. The mark is a crown above the words *Davenport Longport Staffordshire* in puce. This mark, with the lettering in red, was usually associated with Davenport in the period 1870–1880; however the same lettering in puce was also used in the earlier period c. 1830–45.* A remarkably high proportion of this tea service has survived and is on display in the Drawing Room. Two of the sugar basins are still used every Wednesday at the members' weekly luncheon.

Davenport specialised in tea services, with 'Japan' patterns in the early Derby style, two of their painters from the Derby factory being well-known for landscape designs.

At a much later date another dinner service was brought from England, of which some survives and is still in use. The colour scheme remained the same, white with a broad green band, and the mark is *Booths Silicon China England* with a crown. The fact that the marking includes 'England' indicates that it was manufactured after 1891, the inclusion of this word becoming obligatory at that date to comply with the new U.S.A. customs regulations.

Also on display in the Drawing Room is a small collection of black basalt Staffordshire ware, which was bequeathed to the Association by Mr. Maxwell Graham.

Two large teapots, with no maker's name or mark, show on one side a bust of Wellington being crowned with a laurel wreath by Britannia and on the other the inscription 'India, Portugal and Spain, Vittoria 21st June 1813'. A coffee pot has the same marking and wording, with the number 10 embossed on the base. There is also a milk jug, unmarked.

It is possible that these pieces could have been made for a Wedgwood commemorative issue, as has been claimed, but the absence of marking is surprising as Wedgwood ware was almost invariably marked with their name.

Further pieces are a sugar basin and jug, both with lids with handles in the form of a swan and marked on the plinth *EASTWOOD*. This refers to Eastwood Mill at Hanley, Staffordshire, where William Baddeley was described as a maker of black ware and of fancy and ornamental earthenware in the period 1818–22.

*Ref. *Book of British Ceramic Marks*, J. P. Cushion.

Chapter 11

12

Reading Room, Map Room and Writing Room — Interesting items

From the descriptions given so far of the contents of the House, it is interesting to note that whereas all the furniture was made locally, the china was without exception brought from England. This is not surprising, as the standard of work by Portuguese cabinet makers has always been extremely high, whereas the local porcelain or earthenware available, at any rate in the first half of the 19th century, would certainly not have been considered satisfactory for the Factory House, either in design or quality.

Among the many other items in the House, however important and valuable they may be, few if any warrant a separate chapter to themselves, and it is now proposed to discuss the various rooms and to mention at the same time any of their contents that are of interest.

From the earliest days the Reading Room was much patronised and a separate subscription was paid for 'the use of the Newspaper and Billiard Rooms'. This was available to non-members of the Association, but subsequently in 1844 the use of the Billiard Room was denied to them. The earliest list of subscribers is dated 1st January 1816 and it was signed by twenty Subscribers, signifying their agreement to pay Rs. 12$000 (£2 17s. 0d.) per annum in advance. The list contains all the well-known names in the wine trade of that period, the exception being Consul John Crispin who headed the list.

The Reading Room was at first the centre room on the mezzanine floor, where the maps are now hung, and was described in the early inventories as the *Sala das Gazetas*. However by 1847 we find the present writing room called the Reading Room. It was not until 1883 that it was moved to the room at the foot of the staircase from the Library. In 1885 the room until recently used as a library for children's books, facing the street corner of Rua S. João and Rua Infante D. Henrique, was described as the Writing Room.

Originally, when the Factory House was built, it is possible that the mezzanine floor consisted of one long room facing the street, if we can rely on the evidence of a survey made in 1804, which stated that 'The first storey contains a room with seven sash windows'. If this was correct, it means that the four rooms, the present Writing Room, the Map Room, and small corridor adjoining it and the library for children's books, were all joined in one long room, and these four areas do indeed have a total of seven windows.

In the Reading Room a wide selection of local and foreign newspapers and periodicals was available. The first mentioned was the *Lisbon Gazette* in 1812 and in 1816 a subscription was taken out for *The Times, Courier,* Army, Navy and Lloyds Lists and the *Edinburgh* Review. In 1823 came the *Madrid Gazette,* then the *Diario do Governo* (1835), and *Vedeta* (1837). French newspapers were also taken.

The numbers and variety of newspapers, periodicals and magazines that were taken is really remarkable, and in 1870 an invoice from Cowie & Co. in London listed no fewer than 43, including, apart from those mentioned above, the *Morning Post, Daily News, Economist, Bradshaw's Railway Guide, Blackwood's Magazine, Pall Mall Gazette, Boys Magazine* and the *Continental Guide*, all taken on a three-monthly subscription at a total cost of £18 11s. 0d. No doubt without the benefits of radio in those days, not to mention television, the members were avid for all the news and general reading matter that they could get from England and Scotland. *Blackwood's Magazine* was taken from April 1817 with the original issues from the start. *Edinburgh Review* and the *Quarterly Review* were first published in 1802 and 1808 respectively and the back numbers were ordered in 1817.

Stored behind the Writing Room are copies of *The Times* going back to 1832. As already mentioned, the first subscription was taken out in 1816, so possibly for the first 16 years they did not consider it worthwhile to keep them. Framed copies exist of the Trafalgar and Waterloo issues of 7th November 1805 and 22nd June 1815, but these were presented at a later date to the Association. There are also original copies of the *Edinburgh Gazette* and *The Pilot* of 16th October 1810 with Despatches and reports from the Battle of Busaco in which the Portuguese and British armies defeated the French under Massena on 27th September. The ship taking back the Despatches was delayed by bad weather so the news of the victory took some time to reach England.

A copy of *The Times* of one hundred years ago is placed on view every Wednesday in the Drawing Room, where members meet before their weekly luncheon.

Continuing on the mezzanine floor, the centre room with a vaulted ceiling in Moorish style was said to have been called at one time the Contribution Room because on the long narrow table between the pillars in the centre of the room the merchants were thought to have deposited the amounts due by them to the Contribution Fund. There is however no confirmation of this in the records.

The most notable items in this room are the large maps, hung on rollers, that came from England between 1835 and 1837. They include maps of Africa and North & South America, published in 1835 by J. Wyld, of Ireland, Scotland and England & Wales (J. Wyld, 1836) and of Europe (Wyld, 1837). Also a military map of Spain and Portugal re-published in 1836 by Samuel Arrowsmith of 10 Soho Square, London, described as Hydrographer to the King. Another map of Spain and Portugal with a dedication to Lord Somers is undated but is evidently from the 18th century. At a later date in 1854, further maps including one 'Odessa and the Ottoman Empire' were bought from the same James Wyld, of Charing Cross East.

Over the fireplace hangs the well-known map of the River Douro by James Forrester, showing the course of the river from the Spanish frontier to the mouth at Oporto.

Leading out of the Map Room is the Writing Room, with the Visitors' Books dating back to 1812. In these are to be found the names of many officers serving with Wellington's army and with Portuguese regiments during the campaigns in Portugal and Spain. Although one signature is of the Earl of March, described as A.D.C. to the Marquis of Wellington, the signature of Wellington himself is not in the book, and there can be little basis for the

Chapter 12

belief, frequently stated, that he ever visited the Factory House, and dined with the members. When he was in Oporto in 1809 and directed the capture of the city from the French, the Factory House had been abandoned by the members, who had mostly left the country. When they returned in 1811, Wellington was much occupied with the campaign in Spain and is unlikely to have returned again to Oporto.

Also in the Writing Room is a model of the Factory House. Various stories have been told about this and the exact date when it was made is not known. It appears in the 1838 inventory, but was certainly made well before then and it has been said that Consul Whitehead intended to send it to England, possibly to be presented to George III. The model may have been made at the time the Factory House was being built and it is interesting that the balconies were to have been of stone, but in fact were made in iron, which was a novelty at that period.

Also in the Writing Room are two globes, frequently described as having belonged to John Whitehead. This is incorrect and the confusion may have arisen from a reference by Arthur Costigan in 1787 to two globes belonging to Whitehead 'one celestial and one terrestrial, surrounded by a wooden circle four feet in diameter'.

The globes at the Factory House are inscribed 'Malby's Celestial Globe' and are dated 1858, the makers being Thos. Malby & Sons, Parker Street, Little Queen Street, Lincolns Inn Fields, London.

Extract from Visitors' Book, 1812

The origin of the Library ☆ The ground floor ☆ The Gallery ☆ The old Kitchen ☆ The Dining Room

A most important and certainly the most valuable part of the Factory House is the Library.

It is not proposed to discuss or evaluate the contents, which are outside the scope of this work, but some description of the origins of the Library may be of interest.

The Library was not at first owned by the British Association nor housed in the Factory House. It derived from the privately owned 'Oporto Institution', with 14 proprietors mostly port shippers, which, in 1817, requested the use of one of the rooms at the Factory House. There is no record as to where this Institution had its library before nor when it was established. It is probable that the room originally allocated to it was the present writing room, as in the 1838 inventory it was described as 'the room that was the Library'.

After occupying a room in the Factory House an order was placed by the Institution in March 1817, with the London firm Longman, Hurst Rees Orme & Brown for 102 works, to a total of 400 volumes, at a cost of £241 6s. 10d. In May 1818, the year of publication, a first edition of Keats's 'Endymion' was bought for 12s.

But in 1835, when the British Consulate ceased to be situated in the Factory House, it was decided that the rooms formerly occupied by the Consul as his office should be appropriated as the Library. It was also decided 'that it was proper and requisite that every member should have it in his power to subscribe to the Library without undergoing a Ballot or waiting for any form of election'. Previously all subscribers to the Library were subject to proposal and ballot and this continued for many years in the case of non-members: 'Respectable residents being admissible as subscribers by Ballot'.

Early in 1842, a Committee was formed to 'report on the best means of forming a Library to belong to the Association', and as a result the proprietors of the Oporto Institution were approached and they expressed their willingness to dispose of their shares for about £33 each and this offer was accepted. Sixteen member-houses of the Association and one individual member each contributed an equal share to complete the purchase and the total cost of the Library amounted to £465.

It is not entirely clear from the records whether the subscription paid to the Newspaper Room which was established for members in 1850, also included the use of the Library, but by 1856 the number of subscribers had fallen to 12 and from 1857 onwards there is no mention of the Library in the Association accounts, although the Library continued to be managed by a Member called, in 1842 and for many years subsequently, the Treasurer of the Library, but in recent times the Librarian. At which stage the Library occupied the same rooms as at present is not known, but it expanded gradually and it was

recorded as recently as 1923 that the Library was to be enlarged and it
certainly has not been changed since then. According to Sellers in 1899 the
Library contained about 20,000 volumes and this number must have
increased considerably since then, although partially reduced recently as in
accordance with a decision taken at a general meeting of members the
collection of 19th century fiction, amounting to about 2,300 volumes, was
sold in 1982 to the London antiquarian bookseller Bertram Rota.

It is possible that for many years the only part of the ground floor actually
used by the Association was the central hall, described in 1818 as the 'Piazza'
by Mr. Francis Van Zeller, who requested its use for 'the accommodation of
Sedan Chairs this evening'.

The first Fire Insurance Policy dated 1825, taken out with the Phoenix
Insurance Co., states 'there are some small shops on the ground floor, one in
the occupation of a Carpenter'.

This is confirmed by the accounts, which in 1812 and subsequent years
refer to a lodge and a shop on the ground floor rented to two tenants. As late
as 1850 authorisation was given to rent the *Loja* at 24 & 25 Rua S. João.

In a series of articles published in 1967 in the daily newspaper *O Primeiro d
Janeiro* it was stated that 'it was said that Cock fighting took place in a small
room off the hall which had a ring in the centre and a gallery for the
audience'. The source of this was not given and it is open to doubt, the more
so as a great deal in these articles on the subject of the contents of the Factor
House was far from correct.

According to Rebello da Costa there were also stables and coach houses or
the ground floor, and it is possible that these were adjoining the main

building on the west side. Two mahogany doors still exist against a blocked wall, one at the end of the Loggia and the other in the cloakroom. These could have originally opened into the coach house in premises which were subsequently given up.

The principal rooms of the House, situated on the main floor, have really changed very little over the years, with the exception of the Drawing Room which was originally divided into two rooms. When it was made into one room is not certain, but as recently as 1924 the staircase in the corner, immediately to the left on entering the room by the main door, was removed and the present staircase made outside the Drawing Room, leading to the Ladies Room and to the Gallery above the Ballroom and on to the old Kitchen and the Billiard Room.

The Music Gallery was very important in view of the numerous Balls that were held. In 1827 a payment of Rs. 12$000 (£4 14s. 0d.) was made for 'Calling Quadrilles' and in 1836 the Gallery was gilded and benches and light brackets provided for the orchestra. Whether the benches refer to the small narrow seats in mahogany (of an unusual shape and size), which are still in the gallery, is not certain.

Visitors are often surprised to find the old Kitchen at the top of the House. In 1827 Kinsey had commented: 'In Portuguese houses the kitchen is generally situated at the top of the house, so that we became quite accustomed to the expression which so much astonished us at first bring down the dinner, instead of serve the dinner up'. Murphy had also mentioned this in 1795, 'Here no apartment is furnished with a fire-place but the kitchen and this is usually placed in the attic story'. Murphy was writing about his visit before the Factory House was completed, so he was perhaps unaware that several of the rooms were to have fireplaces. One of the earliest documents surviving is a list of the kitchen ranges and utensils that came from England in 1818, together with the china described earlier. Included were jelly moulds, cake and pastry tins, a toasting fork, frying pans and a plate warmer. These are on display now, as is a machine for grinding knives imported in 1861 from Deane & Co., 46 King William Street, London Bridge, at a cost of £9. The same firm supplied a kitchen stove in 1880 for £16 5s. 9d. Of course the Kitchen was in use much earlier, presumably since the House was built, and an entry in 1812 in the cash book records 'Repairing the kitchen grates'. In 1836 a hot closet was installed in the Kitchen.

Complete instructions were given, which still survive for 'fixing the Hot closet and Boiler', showing how the furnace was to be built up with fire bricks, leaving a small escape valve for the steam and how the cold water inlet was to be connected to the main kitchen cistern. The instructions contained the obvious warning to the effect that 'should the Boiler be without water at any time, it will be liable to damage'. The supplier of this range was J. Evans, at King William Street, London Bridge. Further kitchen stoves were imported in 1859 from Deane & Co. in London, a firm that was established at London Bridge as far back as 1700, according to the brand on the furnace door.

Displayed in the Kitchen are leather fire buckets stamped with the date 1790, which were recently discovered and provide confirmation that the Factory House was first in use in that year. Also there are four Windsor brace-back side chairs, previously unrecognised and identified by a visitor Mr. Ralph Cox, antique dealer and furniture expert. The chairs were included in the 1838 inventory.

Chapter 13

View of the old Kitchen

It is not known when the old Kitchen ceased to be used, but the 1885 inventory refers to the large and small kitchens.

In the Dining Room, some of the items that were bought at various dates do not appear to have survived. In 1834 a snuff box, presumably silver, was presented to George Knowsley. In a letter to James Forrester, the uncle of the famous Joseph James Forrester, he said that some of the members had observed that it would be desirable to have a snuff box belonging to the Association to put on the table after dinner for the use of those persons who at that period enjoy a pinch of snuff.

In 1831, there was a large shipment from Liverpool of what was described as 'Hardware' from Robert Todd & Co., Sheffield. Included were dish covers, cake tins of various sizes, ivory-handled knives, dessert knives, one pair silver plate 12 inch fluted candlesticks No. 7163, cost £3 10s. 0d. per pair, one pair silver plate 'Scroll leaf and flower arm, three light Branches made so as to be used for 5 light Branches No. 7293 with silver classic border' cost £7 17s. 6d. the pair.

In 1848, a purchase was made locally of eight Sheffield silver plate dish covers and two Sheffield salvers. These had originally been supplied by Storrs, 106 Cheapside, London, and it was noted that 'The ornaments and feet and handles are of silver, not plate'. The Association paid the equivalent of £50 for these.

Other interesting items are a set of silver-plated salt cellars, with blue liners. Originally twelve, but now only eleven, they appear to date from about 1850 and were included in an inventory of that period, described as *'saleiros ricos com vidro azul'* (rich salt cellars with blue glass). They may possibly be of French origin and are in regular use in the Dining Room.

On display in the Drawing Room are four decanters and a number of wine glasses in green glass, mentioned in the 1847 inventory 'for Hock'. They came from England in 1830 at a cost of 2/- each for the glasses and £1 6s. 0d. each for the decanters. They are considered by experts to be of English origin and the decanters, described in the original account as 'neat cut', to be of high quality.

In the Dining Room is a bracket clock by James Bidlake, London. The maker was a Liveryman of the Clockmakers Company in 1816 and was established at 48 Chiswell Street from 1816–20 and as James Bidlake & Son at the same address until 1845. It would appear that the clock in the Factory House is of the earlier period and was purchased from London in 1835, at the cost of ten guineas and described as a table clock.

Another clock was purchased in 1854 from Brockbank Atkins & Son of Cowpers Court, Cornhill, for £20 and described as 'Large Spring Clock to strike the hours on Bell in square rosewood french polished case, No. 2237'. There is no trace of this clock.

It is interesting that, whereas in the early days the Factory House had little furniture and it became necessary to hire many items, at a later date it was evidently the members who were lacking, because at a meeting on 10th January 1877 it was recorded: 'That great inconvenience having arisen from lending the furniture, etc. a resolution should be passed providing that no article of furniture, plate, glass or linen, the property of the Institution, should be sent out of the House on any pretext whatever. Ballot carried unanimously, the balls being all white'.

The Dining Room

Chapter 13

14 Paintings and Portraits

There are many portraits hanging in the House, for the most part of former members, and they are listed below.

Drawing Room

Elizabeth Graham, née Noble (1808–1889), the daughter of John Hatt Noble (see below), after a painting dated 1836 by J. Graham Gilbert RSA. She married John Graham in 1835.

George Glas Sandeman (1793–1868) and *John Glas Sandeman* (1836–1921), both presented by Sandeman & Co. in 1953.

Sir John Croft Bt. (1778–1862). Son of John Croft (1732–1820), wine merchant at York and author of *Treatise on the Wines of Portugal* 1788, referred to earlier. His family had been associated with Portugal and the port trade since the early part of the 18th century. He was born in Oporto but subsequently resided in England and was not a member of the old Factory. During the Peninsular War he was active in Intelligence work on behalf of the British and Portuguese armies and at the end of the war was appointed by the British Government to administer the relief funds granted to Portugal by Parliament. Created baronet in 1818, Croft was also honoured by the Portuguese with the title Barão de Estrela and appointed Commendador of the Order Torre e Espada, the highest Portuguese decoration.

Andrew James Symington (1863–1939) presented by M. M. Symington.

George Warre (1791–1850). Member of the Association in 1836. Portrait presented by his grandson George F. Warre in 1927.

G. Maxwell Graham. A member 1909–1960 and senior member for many years.

The Revd Samuel Barton DD. Appointed in 1682 by the Bishop of London as 'Preacher to the Factory at Oporto' and expelled by the Inquisition in 1683, as related earlier. Subsequently Chaplain to the Speaker of the House of Commons.

John de Fleurriet Delaforce, the author of this work. Portrait commissioned by the members of the Association and painted in 1987 by Henrique Medina, one of the most distinguished Portuguese portraitists of the 20th century.

Dining Room

John Page (b. Oporto 1699). Portrait attributed to Richard Wilson R.A. (1713–1752), a celebrated landscape painter who worked for some years in Italy and painted Mediterranean scenes in the classical style. Previously he had been apprenticed to a portrait painter in London and his portraits, while not considered of such fine quality as those of his famous contemporary

George Glas Sandeman,
1793–1868

Reynolds, yet achieved some distinction. W. G. Constable (*Richard Wilson*, 1953) considered that the Page portrait, in spite of the traditional attribution, showed some characteristics of the work of Benjamin Wilson (1721–1788) at the end of the 1750s.

Page's father, also John, was in the firm Harris, Page & Pratt at Melgaço & Monção and he built a house at Viana do Castelo in 1703. He was a signatory to a document in 1664 as representing the Lisbon Factory.

The portrait was presented in 1946 by Cecil Page, the great-great grandson of John Page.

John Hatt Noble DL. JP. Described as 'of Leckhampstead & Mortimer in the County of Berks'. Member of the Factory prior to the Peninsular War, of the firm Noble and Murat, British Pro-Consul in 1826. The portrait was presented by G. M. A. Graham in 1929.

John Hatt Noble featured in an interesting story connected with Nelson, reported in the London *Morning Post* of 26th June 1931:

'After Trafalgar, "Victory" put into Gibraltar and furniture in Nelson's cabin, consisting of a mahogany dining table, sideboard and cellarette, was sold by his Steward to Admiral Henry Warre. He sent them to his cousin John H. Noble, then Treasurer of the British Association at Oporto, and left them to him on his death in 1826. They remained in the Noble family until 1862 when they became the property of D. M. Fuerheerd. The latter's grandson sold the pieces at Christie's in 1931 for £997 10s. and the purchaser expressed his intention of presenting them to "Victory".'

John Noble (1746–1828). Described as 'of Mortimer', so possibly the father of John H. Noble above.

Chapter 14

John Graham (1797–1886). Painted in 1823 after the portrait by Richard Carruthers. He has been mentioned earlier as one of the signatories to the Memorial in 1825 on the subject of the ownership of the Factory House.

Sir Robert Newman, Bt. (1776–1848) of Mamhead Park, Devon, and M.P. for Exeter. After the painting by Thomas Phillips R.A. The Newman family was associated with Portugal and the Port Wine trade since the early part of the 18th century, with connections in Dartmouth and Viana do Castelo and the import of *bacalhau* (dried cod) from Newfoundland. Their firm was originally Holdsworth, Olive & Newman, then in 1812 Hunt Newman Roope and finally Hunt Roope & Co. Members of the Newman family are still connected with the trade as owners of Quinta da Eira Velha in the Alto Douro.

William Campion (1738–1818). Partner c. 1800 in Campion, Offley, Hesketh & Co., members of the Factory and predecessors of Offley Forrester & Co.

Reproduction from the portrait by Sir Thomas Lawrence P.R.A., kindly presented by Mr. David Campion from the original at his family home 'Danny' at Hurstpierpoint, Sussex.

Outside the Dining Room	*Thomas Newman* (1785–1866) of Mamhead Park, Devon. Brother of Sir Robert Newman, see above.

Herbert William Pheysey (1872–1934).

Mezzanine Landing

King D. João VI. An unattractive portrait by an unknown artist. He has been mentioned earlier in connection with the abolition of foreign Factories in 1810. In 1807, when he was Prince Regent, he left Portugal for Brazil to escape capture by the French. The British had been urging his departure for some time and provided a warship to escort him. The portrait was presented in 1854 by a member, William G. Roughton, on his election to the Association. He described it as 'an oil painting which he believes to be a moderately good likeness of His late Portuguese Majesty Don John the Sixth'.

King D. João IV (Reign 1640–1656). A portrait of considerable historical interest, as it was during his reign that the important Treaty of 1654 was signed with Cromwell, whereby the establishment of British Factories in Portugal was permitted and commercial and religious privileges granted to the British. It can be said that this date marked the beginning of the special relationship between Portugal and Great Britain which has continued to exist ever since.

Above the Main Staircase

Above the main stairs, outside the Ballroom, hangs the large portrait of Lieutenant-General Sir William Warre. He was born in Oporto in 1784 and joined the firm of Warre & Co., of which his uncle, William Warre, born 1748, was the Senior Partner. He did not remain long in the wine trade, being dismissed from the firm, so the story goes, for fastening the pigtail of one of the Portuguese staff to his desk with sealing wax, when he was having an after-lunch nap. He was sent to a private tutor at Bonn to prepare for an army career and in 1803 at the age of 19 received a commission in the 52nd Light Infantry, under the command of Sir John Moore. Subsequently he served as A.D.C. to General Ferguson at the battles of Roliça and Vimeiro and later as principal A.D.C. to General Beresford. He took part in the famous retreat from Corunna. He saw much service in the Peninsular War, including

the passage of the Douro in 1809 and the battle of Salamanca, the assault of Ciudad Rodrigo and the sieges of Badajos. For his services in Portugal he was awarded the Order of the Tower and Sword and of St Bento d'Avis. His distinguished career continued with appointments in England and Ireland, with a final command of the Northern District stationed at York. He was knighted in 1839.

General Warre was the grandson of William Warre, born 1706, who had joined the firm Clark & Thornton in 1729 and who married Elizabeth Whitehead, the sister of John Whitehead. It was the latter's nephew, another William Warre, who was appointed Consul in Oporto in 1802, and who was said to have taken the Factory records to England in 1807.

The portrait of General Warre is a copy of the original painting by William M. Craig, R.A., in the ownership of Major Anthony Warre in London.

Consul John Whitehead. A full-length portrait of John Whitehead shows him seated at a table holding a parchment scroll on which can be read the words 'British Cemetery' and 'Weights and Measures'. These are references to the

Chapter 14

establishment of the first Protestant cemetery in Oporto in 1787 as a result of his influence and to the system of water measurement said to have been invented by him and adopted by the local authorities in Lisbon and Oporto. The picture was cleaned and restored in 1907 by Eduardo de Moura, a well-known Portuguese artist, and it was then recorded that the canvas bore the name of W. Legg, High Holborn, London, and the date 1802. This was presumably the supplier of the canvas. When the picture was again cleaned in January 1979 it was noted that the frame bore the name of James Bourlet & Sons Ltd., Fine Art Packers and Frame Makers of Nassau Street, London W. This firm still exists in London.

It had been assumed that the portrait was painted probably in England, before Whitehead's death in December 1802. It is now known however that in fact it was painted after his death. In accordance with a resolution taken at a Factory meeting the day after his death (reproduced in part on page 19) the late Consul's family were requested 'to permit a Painting to be taken of him from the best likeness in their possession, to be placed in the Factory House'. As Whitehead had been living in Oporto for forty-six years, it is logical to assume that the best likeness would have been more easily available at Oporto. The fact that the canvas and the frame are of London origin is of little relevance, as an artist in Portugal at that time would very likely have obtained both from England. There is no signature on the painting, but only the inscription 'S.L. facit'. So the identity of the artist remains unknown.

Whitehead died on 15th December 1802 and was buried in the British Cemetery on the 18th. The members of the Factory House resolved 'that the remains of the late John Whitehead Esq. our much respected Consul be interr'd on Saturday the 18th instant at 12 o'clock in the Centre of the Burial Ground and in deviating of the established Rule in respect to his memory. [This refers to the regulation that no inscription was to be put on any grave-stone; see page 28.] That a handsome and most expressive monument be erected, at the expense of the Factory, and it being the desire of the Factory to pay every possible attention, that the Treasurer consult the wishes of his Nephew William Warre Esq. on this occasion'.

In fact it was several years before the monument was made in England and it took the form of an urn surmounting a base on which an inscription in Latin records his date and place of birth and pays tribute to his fine qualities.

Between the portraits of John Whitehead and General Warre, above the staircase, hangs a picture with an interesting history, although the circumstances in which it was presented to the Factory House remain uncertain.

The artist was Francisco Vieira Portuense 1765–1805, and the painting depicts Edward I and Queen Eleanor in Palestine at the time of the Crusades, with the Queen sucking the poison out of a wound inflicted on the King by a poisoned dagger. Vieira, one of the best known Portuguese artists of the latter part of the 18th century, was born in Oporto, and son of Domingos Francisco Vieira, who has been described as a mediocre provincial painter of landscapes in the style of Pillement, the well-known French artist who was said to have taught the Vieiras, both father and son. However, young Vieira must have shown some early promise as he, together with Domingos António Sequeira, another well-known Portuguese painter of that period, were awarded grants in 1788 by the Companhia das Vinhas do Alto Douro to go to Rome to study under the Italian, Domenico Corvi. There they received the patronage of the

[78]

William Warre (1706–76)
from a painting by Hugh
Barron, 1771

Portuguese Ambassador Melo e Castro and Vieira was able to establish his own studio and to travel extensively in Italy, notably to Parma to study the paintings of Correggio, as well as to Venice, Verona, Mantua and Padua and many other cities. In 1797 Vieira went to Germany and painted in Dresden, Munich and Berlin, finally reaching London the same year, where he was to stay for several years. In London, his patron Melo e Castro had been appointed Ambassador to the Court of St James and he was able to renew his friendship with Francesco Bartolozzi, the famous Florentine engraver who was one of the original members of the Royal Academy and whom Vieira had known in Rome. He subsequently married a niece of Bartolozzi.

In this artistic circle, Vieira was able to meet some of the famous painters of the day, including Reynolds and Angelica Kauffmann (1741–1807). Vieira was much influenced by the latter, an artist of some renown in both Rome and London who specialised in historical subjects, although Vieira himself was to become known for his paintings of religious subjects, of which there are several examples in Portugal.

Angelica Kauffmann painted the original work from which Vieira took his

[79]

Chapter 14

Worcester Vase in Drawing Room (Angelica Kauffmann painting)

theme for the painting in the Factory House, although the latter shows considerable differences in interpretation and the scene is portrayed in a more romantic style than the classicism of the original. The latter had been exhibited at the Royal Academy in 1776.

Two sources refer to Vieira's picture being in the Factory House. The Oporto periodical *O Tripeiro*, in an article published in 1909, recorded that one of Vieira's best works, depicting a British historical scene, is in the Factory House and referred to one other historical work by him in the style of Angelica Kauffmann.

A second reference can be found in the study of Vieira Portuense in *A arte em Portugal no século XIX* by José Augusto França (Oporto, 1966), which records that the painting 'Edward I of England and Eleanor of Castille' was directly inspired by a well-known work of Angelica Kauffman and was offered to the Feitoria Inglesa, having been painted in London in 1798.

Vieira returned to Oporto towards the end of 1800 and received official appointments both there and in Lisbon, where he was nominated as Court Painter, but his health had been deteriorating and for this reason he went to Madeira where he died in 1805 at the age of forty.

The picture was cleaned and restored in July 1980 and this revealed the signature and date 'F. Vieira inv. 1798'. The letters 'inv.' are an abbreviation of the Portuguese word *inventou*, signifying that the picture was inspired by the work of another artist.

Thus the authenticity of the painting is confirmed, although there is no definite evidence of the circumstances in which it came to the Factory House. It has been said that Vieira was given financial assistance to pursue his studies in Italy by the British Factory collectively or by some of the British Merchants. Recent research by Art Historian Paulo Varela Gomes in Lisbon into the life and work of Vieira has produced evidence that appears to confirm this. Letters from the Portuguese Ambassador in Rome, referred to earlier, written in August and September 1789, mentioned that Vieira was in receipt of grants from his parents and 'from some foreigners resident in Oporto'.

It was rather ironical if Vieira was financed by the Companhia as well as by the Factory, as has been claimed, as these two bodies were vigorously opposed to one another.

However another source has been quoted as having the conviction, based on some correspondence from Vieira, that he was not sent to Italy by the Companhia, as contemporary tradition maintained, but by the British Merchants. (Ref: Francisco Cordeiro Blanco *Boletim do MNAA*, 1 (3) 1948 pp. 149/51.)

There are two possible explanations as to how the painting came into the possession of the Factory House. Either Vieira presented it, in gratitude for the assistance that had been given to him, choosing a picture with a theme that is historically appropriate for a British Institution, or else merchants in London with Oporto connections bought it after it was exhibited at the Royal Academy in 1798 and then presented it to the Factory House. It could have been those mentioned by Joseph Farrington, Secretary of the Royal Academy, in his diary, as a group of London merchants who called themselves 'The Lisbon & Oporto Club of Merchants' and who met on the first Thursday of every month in a London pub.

The Factory House painting was loaned in 1987/8 to exhibitions of Portuguese Art in Paris and Lisbon.

An interesting link with the Vieira painting is the very fine Worcester vase on display in the Drawing Room. Inside the cover is written 'Edward & Eleanora' and the maker's name: Chamberlains, Worcester, Porcelain Manufacturers to HRH The Prince Regent. This dates the vase in the period 1811–20. The painting reproduced is that by Angelica Kauffmann described above. Her works were much used for reproduction on the Worcester porcelain, especially vases, at that period.

The vase was in the ownership of Andrew James Symington, a member of the Association, and was presented to the Factory House by his family after his death.

Map Room

There are two photographs of 18th-century British Chaplains to the Factory.

One is of a portrait attributed to Richard Wilson of the Reverend Henry Wood, Chaplain at Oporto 1757–1768. He has been mentioned earlier in connection with the building of the Santo António Hospital.

The other is of a miniature of the Reverend William Emmanuel Page, dated 1766. Page was Chaplain to the British Factory 1768–76. He was born in Oporto, being baptised in 1738 by the Chaplain to the Factory, the Revd John Nichols. His parents were John Page and Ann Dowker, she the daughter of Peter Dowker, merchant at Oporto and founder of the firm Lambert Kingston & Co. The father has been mentioned earlier in connection with his portrait by Richard Wilson. The Revd Page was later to be Prebendary of Chester Cathedral 1796–1801. The photograph was presented by Sir Ralph Newman in 1956.

Also in the House are nine prints of portraits of the British royal family, Queen Victoria, King Edward VII and Queen Alexandra, King George V and Queen Mary, King George VI and Queen Elizabeth, and Queen Elizabeth II and Prince Philip, Duke of Edinburgh. The two latter were presented to the Association by the Queen after her visit in 1957. All the prints are signed, except for those of Queen Victoria, King George VI and Queen Elizabeth.

The Factory House at Oporto

15

Entertainments at the Factory House ☆ Receptions for Royalty and other Distinguished Visitors

The Factory House was frequently the scene of formal Balls which were held regularly and whenever distinguished visitors came to Oporto, including Portuguese royalty on several occasions. It was all done in the grand manner, the first Ball being in 1812 in honour of the Prince of Orange. For Marshal Beresford in 1819 military music was provided and at a Ball in 1827 a regimental band. At the Ball for the Portuguese royal family in 1835 there was a guard, an escort of cavalry, a military band and even 'gloves for the soldiers'. The Prince de Lippe in 1824 had been honoured with a Ball and a Dinner, while in 1842 the birth of HRH The Prince of Wales (later King Edward VII) was celebrated with a Ball.

Kinsey had written of 'the resident merchants of the British Factory giving public entertainments to persons of their own class and to the Portuguese families of consequence, such as Balls in the winter and occasional dances'. The functions were certainly not public in the sense that the members seem to have been very exclusive with their invitations and the programme of the Balls to be given during the coming season was usually decided at the first members' meeting of the year each January and a small committee was nominated for the organisation and management of each Ball. On the more important occasions the list of guests to be invited was agreed at a meeting of members. At such a meeting in 1819 it was decided that 'No Portuguese officer under the rank of Field-Officer can be invited'.

Several writers were loud in their praises of the hospitality they received in Oporto.

Major William Dalrymple, writing of his travels through Spain and Portugal in 1774, described how 'he feasted most voluptuously with the Consul and the Factory who were remarkably civil and attentive'. Significantly he did not mention the existence of any Factory House.

Kinsey, at a later date, was also appreciative of the hospitality in Oporto, which he described as 'far to be preferred to that of Lisbon'.

Henry Frederick Link wrote about the Factory House in *Travels in Portugal 1797–1799* (London, 1801): 'They have a kind of cafino (sic) in a handsome building which is extremely well regulated'.

Lord Carnavon, in an account of his journey to Oporto in 1827 (*Portugal and Galicia*, London 1836) expressed 'his best thanks to Mr. Crispin, the British Consul, who hospitably offered me apartments at his house and showed me every attention during my residence in that city. To my banker, Mr. Kingston, and to the gentlemen of the Factory of whose civilities I am highly sensitive'.

Harrison, writing in 1839, was evidently well entertained, 'nor are the hospitalities of the British Factory to be forgotten. If we may speak on our own experience, we should say that the private cellars of some of the Oporto

[83]

merchants contain wines of a quality rarely, if ever, met with in England. Of all the towns in Portugal, Oporto is that in which the Englishman will find himself most at home. He will there, if he have the advantage of an introduction, be literally overwhelmed with invitations from the British merchants resident in the city'.

It is interesting to note that the term 'Factory' was still in use twenty-nine years after it had been officially abolished.

Six years later, Kingston was to write on the same subject, but in a rather more snobbish vein. 'There are at Oporto two assembly rooms which the higher classes frequent. The oldest is the British Association, commonly called the English Factory House, established some fifty years ago by twelve or rather more of the principal British merchants of the city. At one time the fidalgos only with few exceptions were invited there, including the chief military and civil authorities in the place with their families. Now however it would be impossible to keep up such a distinction and consequently all respectable families who mix in the general society of the place are in turn invited'.

Finally on this subject, J. Valente Perfeito was more specific a century later 'It is not in vain that the British Association in Oporto enjoys the reputation of serving the finest Ports in the world, and with the right food too. If you are not fortunate enough to have enjoyed a well matured Stilton with a robust Vintage Port at the Factory, or elsewhere for that matter, you have certainly missed something in your life'.

Even the wives of the members had been excluded from the dinners, and it was not until 22nd August 1843, on the occasion of the visit to Oporto by the first Bishop of Gibraltar, that in the words of a recorded minute 'it is worthy of remark that this is the first occasion on which Ladies have been invited to dine at the Factory House'. The Bishop had come to consecrate the British Chapel which had been built 25 years previously. There were evidently subtle shades of meaning between the various entertainments. The most important and ceremonious were the Balls, which obviously the ladies attended. Then there were less formal dances or parties and it was to the latter that the ladies were first invited in 1831. A minute recorded: 'Resolved that a party be given to the Ladies on Tuesday evening the 18th January 1831'.

Finally, the ultimate honour was to be invited to a dinner and it was this that the ladies only achieved in 1843.

Evidently the members found the presence of the ladies to their liking, as in December the same year the House Committee invited 80 persons to tea, including wives, and the invitation list contained the names of many well-known Oporto families, such as Van Zeller, Villar, Saavedra, Teixeira de Mello, Brito e Cunha, Kopke and Allen.

However things have not changed much during the intervening 140 years, and ladies rarely attend dinners or even lunches at the Factory House, although it is true that a mixed lunch is held every three months or so.

The Balls given in honour of the kings of Portugal in 1861 and 1863 were very lavish affairs. At the former the attendance was 580, while at the latter for which no numbers are recorded, the total cost of about £400 was double that of the previous Ball.

There were obviously no safety regulations in force at that time as regards the Ballroom floor. This was inspected in recent times and it was recommended that the maximum number that could safely use the floor was about 300 persons. Possibly the modern dances are more violent, but it might be thought that the polkas and waltzes that predominated one hundred years ago would have placed just as much strain on the floor.

At the 1861 Royal Ball, there was a guard of honour of 15 infantry and eight cavalry, and 'His Majesty graciously opened the Ball and his brother danced several times'. The supper provided included eight turkeys, of which it was noted that two had gone bad, 40 chickens, 12 duck, 24 pigeons and 25 quail. The food seemed to be mostly meat, game and poultry, with a small amount of soles, lobsters and turbot, and finally sweets, for which 300 eggs were used.

In 1863, there were 53 manservants and waiters on duty, as well as the head chef, the latter paid £5 per day, and eight assistants, together with six ladies' maids and four women to supervise the flower arrangements.

On these occasions, it was the custom for servants to be lent by the leading Oporto families and those recorded were, Cobb, Delaforce, Fladgate, Graham, Noble, Roope, Sandeman, Smithes, Teage and Wright. Also the Consul and the Doctor lent servants as well as the Baronezas de Vilaverde & de Vilar, and the firms Ferreirinha, Rebello Valente & Borges. This custom had been observed from the early days and at one of the first meetings of members in 1811 it was decided 'that each member of the Society be required to send a servant to attend on the Assembly nights'.

The menu in 1863 was very similar to that on the previous royal occasion except that a peacock, costing £3, was provided. The smallest items of expenditure were 'two tortoise combs for the King & Queen', cost £1.

However magnificent the occasion was by Factory House standards, it paled into insignificance compared with the Ball to the King & Queen on 24th November 1863 at the *Associação Comercial*, when 4,000 guests were present and the 1785 port was served.

There was another visit to the Factory House by Portuguese Royalty in 1908 when King D. Manuel II accepted an invitation to luncheon.

In fact the minutes recorded that he was entertained to breakfast, accompanied by his Prime Minister, Foreign Minister and other members of the Government. The Bishop of Oporto was also present.

'He used the same pen to write his signature that had been provided for the Kings of Portugal on their previous visits and a silver inkstand given by King D. Carlos to George Dagge, whose sons Richard and John presented it to the Factory House in 1957.'

D. Manuel, the last King of Portugal was deposed on the proclamation of the Republic in 1910 and went into retirement in England. He had become King following the assassination in Lisbon in February 1908 of his father D. Carlos, and of his elder brother.

The only visit to the Factory House by a British monarch was on the 21st February 1957 when Her Majesty Queen Elizabeth II, accompanied by Prince Philip, came to Oporto at the conclusion of their official visit to Lisbon. Unfortunately the stay was of very short duration, in fact Her Majesty was less than a half an hour in the House, but there was time for the members and others of the British Community to be presented to her and she was able to taste the finest Factory House port.

A more recent royal visit was on 22nd May 1979 when Her Royal Highness The Princess Anne, accompanied by her husband Captain Mark Phillips, paid an official visit to Oporto. A reception was held at the Factory House, attended by the British Community in the north of Portugal, at which many were presented to Her Royal Highness, who was shown over the House during her stay of about one and a half hours. On her departure she was much applauded by the large crowd that had gathered in the street to see her

On the occasion of the first visit to Portugal by a British Prime Minister in office, a reception for the British Community was held on 19th April 1984 in honour of the Right Hon. Mrs. Margaret Thatcher FRS MP. She was accompanied by Dr. Mário Soares, the Portuguese Prime Minister who subsequently became President, and in that capacity dined with the Treasurer and Members on 26th October 1988, the first Portuguese head of state to visit the Factory House for 80 years. A previous President, General Carmona, had accepted an invitation to dinner in July 1940, but later regretted that circumstances made it impossible for him to come to Oporto.

The most recent Royal visit was on 14th February 1987 when HRH The Prince and Princess of Wales attended a reception held during the celebrations marking the sixth centenary of the wedding in the Cathedral in Oporto of King John I and Philippa of Lancaster.

Among the many visitors to the Factory House over the years, mention is made later of the entertainment offered on various occasions to the officers of Royal Navy ships calling at Oporto. These visits continued regularly into the present century, although they have tended to become less frequent in recent times and on a smaller scale, sadly reflecting the present day reduction in the size and importance of the Royal Navy.

One of these early naval visits was by the cricket XI of the Channel Squadron in March 1869, the first recorded match in Oporto against a team from abroad. On this occasion Oporto were dismissed for 17 runs. The Channel Squadron were entertained to dinner at the Factory House and in the following year, during another visit to Portugal by the same Squadron, 'The Admiral, Captains, Commanders and their Officers from each vessel now in the Tagus' attended a 'Ball & Supper'.

Since then there have been many cricket matches in Oporto against visiting teams from England and elsewhere, who have included M.C.C., Cryptics, Dorset Rangers, Gentlemen of Worcester, Eton Ramblers, Wine Trade Sports Club, Gibraltar Cricket Club and Law Society and the old rival Lisbon, against whom matches have been played annually for over a hundred years. All these teams were entertained at the Factory House.

Of greater significance, in the context of the port wine trade, have been the official visits to Oporto in 1928, 1966 and 1978 by the Masters, Wardens and Members of the Court of the Worshipful Company of Vintners who on each occasion were received at the Factory House.

16 Customs and Accommodation at the Factory House

Until the middle of the 19th century, it was the custom to hold a breakfast on the day of the procession of Corpus Christi. In 1845 there were 50 persons present and the cost of the refreshments, exclusive of wines but including the hire of curtains for the windows, amounted to £5. The consumption of wine was below average, but included two bottles of port each from Hunt, Sandeman & Fladgate.

The custom of watching the procession on that day was observed also by the British in Lisbon, and Robert Southey in 1797 had been shocked not only by the nature of the processions, particularly in the more violent times of the Inquisition, but also by the fact that the British should have watched them. He quoted a lady as saying 'The English whose houses overlooked the streets through which they passed kept open house and made entertainment'.

During the 16th century, if not earlier, the procession had passed along the Rua Nova, where the Factory House now stands, and down to the riverside of the Ribeira. But early in the 17th century the Bishop of Oporto petitioned the King that the route should be changed on the grounds that some of the streets along which it passed were 'indecent', especially at the Ribeira where 'fish was sold'. The King at first agreed to the request, but stipulated that the itinerary should continue to include the 'Rua Nova, the best street in the City'. However the Town Council then asked the King to leave things as they were, as otherwise there would be complaints from the residents in those streets through which the procession had always passed, and he replied to them that he was instructing the Bishop that things should be left as they were. It is interesting that the Corpus Christi procession first took place in Lisbon as early as 1387.

A traditional event to be held each year at the Factory House is the Treasurer's Dinner. This function, attended exclusively by the members, dates back to the early part of the 19th century and is required to be voted at the first meeting of members each January. The dinner was originally held in January, to compliment the new Treasurer who had just taken office. Later it was held at any time of the year, at the discretion of the Treasurer, and in recent years usually in November. Except in 1939 & 1940, during the Second World War, the Dinner appears to have taken place every year since its inauguration. At the Treasurer's Dinner in 1947 the British Ambassador and the Treasurer were suffering from colds and they left the room to gargle with Port before the speeches and it was recorded that it proved most beneficial and efficacious to both of them. It is in fact an excellent remedy for the relief of a cold or sore throat.

The members meet for lunch every Wednesday, when guests can be invited. The attendance usually numbers about thirty. Prior to the Second

World War, the members lunched at the Factory House on several days a week, but this was discontinued as the attendance gradually declined. Wednesday was considered the most suitable day as in those days most of the firms were shipping mainly to the United Kingdom and as the post by surface mail arrived without fail by train from England in exactly three days, this meant that no correspondence was likely to arrive on a Wednesday. So the shippers would have less to do at their offices and could take their time over lunch at the Factory House and in fact they often did not return to Vila Nova. This certainly does not apply now and although the post today takes considerably longer by airmail than it did before the last war by train yet the automatic telephone and telex demand constant attention and do not respect Wednesday afternoons.

The vintage port for the luncheons is selected by the Treasurer, but the year and shipper are not divulged until those present have had an opportunity to give their opinions. There is such a wide range of vintages in the Factory House cellars, including some of years not generally declared as a vintage, and others of single *quintas*, that it is no easy task to name it correctly and in fact for anyone to name both the year and the shipper correctly is rare, although many present are considered experts. It is noticeable, both now and in the past, that those who have acquired a reputation as very knowledgeable tasters are often those most reluctant to express a firm opinion.

At lunch, no smoking is permitted until after 2p.m. and then only with the permission of the Treasurer or in his absence of the senior member present. This custom is however not always observed nowadays. No speeches are allowed, except in the most exceptional cases, when the Treasurer might propose a toast on some special occasion.

The table used for lunch seats a maximum of 36 in any degree of comfort. Some writers have put the number higher, and Sellers even went as far as sixty.

When possible some distinguished visitor, such as the British Ambassador to Lisbon, is invited to attend the Treasurer's Dinner. One of the earliest Ambassadors to be invited was George Canning in 1815 and there was a proposal that he should use the Factory House as his residence during his stay in Oporto, but it was considered by the majority of members that the House was 'unfit for his acceptance', thus providing further evidence that the furnishings of the House at that date must have been extremely sparse.

On the other hand, travellers visiting Oporto at an earlier date praised the accommodation provided at the Factory House. Lady Holland in 1808 recorded 'We removed from our wretched posada to the inn built in the Factory House for the accommodation of English travellers, spacious, clean and possessing the comforts of fireplaces'. It is remarkable that she should have found it so comfortable, at a time when most of the members were absent and even more that British travellers should have visited Oporto without any qualms during a period when most of the foreign residents evidently considered conditions to be too dangerous for their safety.

A few years later in 1811 William Granville Eliot wrote that 'The Rua Nova where most of the members of the British Factory reside, has two excellent inns in it, the one called the Factory House, supported by the Merchants'.

It is hard to envisage where in the building could have been the rooms that justified such a description. Presumably the bedrooms must have been on the floor above the old Kitchen, in the attics, and the 'inn' may have been managed, for his own account, by the *mordomo* or steward.

However the evidence, in 1825, of John Franklin, described as 'Merchant, at one time of the British Nation', gives the impression that the inn was for a time entirely outside the Factory control or management. He declared that 'on the invasion of the Kingdom by the French and for a short time after, the Building was turned into a Hostelry with an eating house for all travellers of the Nation, and there was also a public Coffee Room at the entrance to the building managed by a man of the name of Queiroz, where every and any person might be provided with drinks, also free admission to English Captains and Clerks to go there and read the public papers in the room set aside for that purpose and it is also within the memory of the witness that sales by public auction were held in the said house under the Arches at the entrance where the English merchants desired to establish them instead of in the street as was the custom. But they were not able to carry out their wish as the Portuguese merchants would not join them, seeing that the Building was English and not National'.

Confirmation that in fact the above mentioned Queiroz was connected with the Factory at that period comes from a receipt signed on 22nd June 1811 by José Vincente de Queiroz. This was on a bill for repainting the '3 Arms of the Allied Nations and of the Prince Regent of Great Britain' on the occasion of the Ball held that month. Queiroz signed the receipt on behalf of the painter António José Vieira. However the use of the House as an hotel ceased in the second half of 1811 as a minute of a meeting on 9th December of that year recorded 'That the Society being unwilling that the Factory House should be used as an Hotel, shall permit João Domingos Nogueira to derive all the benefit that may arise from the Balls, Billiards and Coffee Room and that he shall be allowed to live with his family in the house'. He was in effect the Manager of the Factory House, with considerable perks, in the same way as Queiroz had been, except that visitors were no longer allowed to stay there.

Agostinho Rebello da Costa had written in 1789 that rooms in the Factory House were going to be rented, this in reference to the ground floor, and that there would be apartments for distinguished travellers of all nations.

In the event, Canning never paid his intended visit to Oporto and on his departure from Lisbon in 1816, he wrote to the Consul in Oporto of 'the sincere regret which I feel at being obliged to leave that intention unaccomplished. Circumstances have fallen out very untowardly. Last year my preparations for the journey were actually made: when Buonaparte's reappearance put an end to all peaceful projects'. He sent his respectful good wishes to the Gentlemen at Oporto together with 'my disappointment at not having found an opportunity of becoming personally acquainted with so eminent and interesting an Establishment of British subjects'.

The members must have also been very disappointed that Canning never visited Oporto, because he was certainly one of the most eminent of the Ambassadors appointed to Lisbon. At the time there was expectation that the Prince Regent was about to return from Brazil, and the British Government considered it essential that they should be represented by an Ambassador of the highest possible standing, our good relations with Portugal being of paramount importance in British foreign policy at that time.

However the King, as he had become in 1816, did not return until 1821 and Canning's Mission became purposeless. He requested that he should relinquish his appointment, which had been the subject of much criticism in

Parliament from the Whig opposition, who claimed that his embassy was too costly and on too lavish a scale. Canning had already been Foreign Secretary before his term in Lisbon and was destined to be so again later and subsequently Prime Minister. Certainly no other Ambassador to Lisbon has ever held such high office.

To conclude this second part of the Factory House story, two items of a rather different nature may be of interest.

The first occurred in 1840, when the Association gave a subscription towards the erection of the monument at Pampelido about ten miles north of Oporto, on the site above the beach usually called Mindelo where D. Pedro had landed in July 1832 with his daughter Maria and the Liberal army. This was the prelude to the defeat of the forces under his brother D. Miguel and the subsequent proclamation of D. Maria II as Queen of Portugal in 1834.

Finally, on a lighter note an event unique in the history of the Factory House took place in May 1876 when an exhibition of roses was held. Four of the members, Pedro Fladgate, W. Sharman Crawford, George H. Delaforce and Joseph James Forrester, had requested the use of the House for the exhibition, being 'greatly interested in Horticulture, more particularly at this season of the year in the Queen of Flowers'.

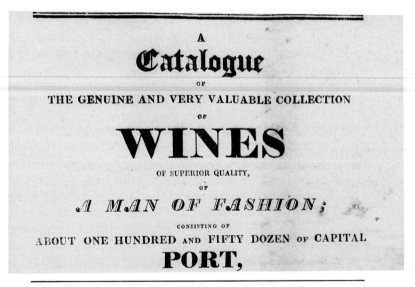

A

Catalogue

OF

THE GENUINE AND VERY VALUABLE COLLECTION

OF

WINES

OF SUPERIOR QUALITY,

OF

A MAN OF FASHION;

CONSISTING OF

ABOUT ONE HUNDRED AND FIFTY DOZEN OF CAPITAL

PORT,

Christie catalogue, 10th August 1815

The Factory House at Oporto

A general view of the Drawing Room

Chapter 16

17

Early cellars ☆ Wines and spirits available ☆ Consumption at Balls

The consumption of wines and spirits, and the variety of drinks available at the Factory House during the 19th century, seem to have been considerably larger than at the present day.

No definite system or pattern emerges as to how the port was provided in the early days, but for many years it was contributed free by the members, but not solely by the Treasurer of the year. In the cellarbook for 1831, the oldest cellar record surviving, there were 12 bins listed. Of these, seven bins contained the ports of 11 individual shippers, namely Roope, Teage, Forrester, Hely, Gonne, Kingston, Greig, Harris, Sandeman, Page and Knowsley. There were two bins of *Lote Novo* and two of *Lote Velho*. The remaining bin contained Madeira. There was no indication as to the composition of the blends of the *Lotes* nor from which shippers they came.

There were also cases in the cellar containing Champagne, Claret, Hock, Barsac and also four dozen Port 'sent by a shipper in 1822'. Other cases contained 'Bucelas, bottled off a hogshead'.

For each dinner or Ball, a few shippers would each contribute a quantity of port and some was also used, for the larger entertainments, from the *Lotes*. The consumption on most occasions averaged about one bottle of port per person, plus large amounts of Champagne, Claret and Madeira.

White port was evidently not highly regarded, but the earliest purchase recorded was in 1819 when 4½ almudes (about 12½ dozen) were supplied by Sandeman and paid for by the Factory House. White port, at this time and on later occasions, was used for culinary purposes, including wine jelly, which was very popular.

In 1843 the cellars were enlarged and the purchase of '10 slate slabs for the cellar' was recorded. This resulted in a greatly increased variety of ports being available and from 1845 onwards there were at times eight ports from different shippers provided for entertainments.

From the *Red Port Wine Cellar Book* started in 1843, we learn little as to whether the ports supplied were vintage wines of one year or blends of various years. The only dates given were the years the wines were binned and the withdrawals for dinners and other functions. Comments on the wines were sadly very few, but a port from J. H. Noble rebinned in 1843 was described as 'very old and thin'. One from Gould & Co. binned in 1838 was 'stout' and another from James Forrester was 'very old'. A Sandeman was bottled in the spring of 1849, binned in 1851 and drunk between 1854–57. A port from James Forrester described as 'fit for immediate use' was binned in 1838, rebinned in 1843 and, surprisingly, drunk over a period as long as 1843–58. From this evidence, it can be seen that the preference was for wines that had been in bottle for some years, but not always for sufficient time to suggest that they were vintage ports in the present sense of the expression.

An interesting entry said that the bottles of a port from Robert Graham Jr. in 1852 were 'waxed', the only instance of such a practice mentioned in the early cellar books. Another significant entry was of ports from John Allen binned in 1839, of which three dozen described as 1804 were marked with 'one cut in the cork', three dozen 1815 with 'two cuts' and seven and a half dozen 'very old' with 'three cuts'. This is the only reference in early records to a vintage date.

The first recorded purchase of any wine or spirit was two almudes (50 litres) of brandy in December 1811.

Madeira was popular and was imported in hogsheads from 1818 and regularly until the middle of the century. Types mentioned were 'Most Superior East India' and Sercial.

Champagne was imported from 1824 and in fair quantities, as much as 56· dozen at a time.

Claret was very popular and was imported from 1822, including top growths such as Château Margaux and Château Lafite.

Sherry was available from 1834, imported in butt, and was often used in the Kitchen. Other drinks available were Hock, Moselle, Cognac, Sauternes, Jamaica Rum (1812), Cherry Brandy (1830), and Lisbon Wine (1846). The first mention of 'Whiskey' was in 1846, but a note said it was bought locally and not imported direct. Gin was only mentioned much later, in 1880.

There are few references to Portuguese table wines by name except for Bucellas which was bought by the hogshead in 1825 and in subsequent years, and frequently served at dinners. Later in 1877 a mention of Collares appears and in 1888 of 'Monção wine', the latter being *Vinho Verde*.

At Balls given in honour of the Portuguese royal family no local table wines were evidently considered good enough to serve to the guests. At one in September 1861 to 'El Rei D. Pedro V and S.A.R. D. João Duque de Beja' (the King's brother) 90 bottles of champagne were consumed together with various quantities of Sherry, Claret, Lisbon Wine and Madeira, as well as 72 bottles of Porto Velho Superior. The local table wines, to the extent of 75 bottles, were however used to make Sangrias and 'for the musicians and soliders'. At times port was also used to make Sangrias.

Supplies for the dinners and Balls were bought locally and in 1863 from the apparently British owned shop of Stephen Whistler, a wine merchant. Beer was bought at 8s. per dozen and champagne at 8s. per bottle. Whistler stocked Pale Ale from Allsops & Bass & Co., Dark from Barclay Perkins and Dublin Stout from 'Guiness & Co.'. He also sold Cognac, Rum, English Gin, Hollands Gin, 'Sauterne', Sherry and Port.

Whistler had evidently established himself in Oporto not long before, as in 1855 he had been introduced as a guest at the Factory House, with his address given as London.

At some dinners the consumption of wines was very high and in 1863 when the officers of H.M.S. *Cyclops*, Steam Frigate, were entertained, 97 bottles of various wines were consumed by 33 persons, including 30 bottles of port.

The next year, for the officers of H.M.S. *Gladiator*, 40 persons consumed 90 bottles, including 32 of port. At another dinner to the officers of 'The Squadron on this Station', with 38 present, they consumed 42 bottles of port supplied by Sandeman, Kingston, Forrester and Warre.

On the other hand, at an earlier date in 1848, with 44 ladies present out of a total of 106, the consumption of port was 'only' 41 bottles, so evidently the ladies were a restraining influence.

Although it was usual for the port to be taken from the stock in the Factory House, and so presumably bottled for some time, yet there is a reference to a Ball in 1849 when 91 bottles of port were consumed 'newly bottled for the purpose' (shipper Sandeman). Normally the port was supplied by several members but at the Ball to Her Majesty in 1852 the port was presented by one member firm alone (Lambert & Noble).

Apart from wines there are records of Beer (1818) and Pale Ale being imported and also Soda and Malvern Seltzer Waters, the latter from J. Schweppe & Co. of Berners Street, London, while York ham, cheeses, mustard and biscuits were similarly brought from England. A stilton cheese was imported in 1831 from Peter Sowerby, Cheese Factor of 22 Castle Street Liverpool, at a cost of 15s. 3d.

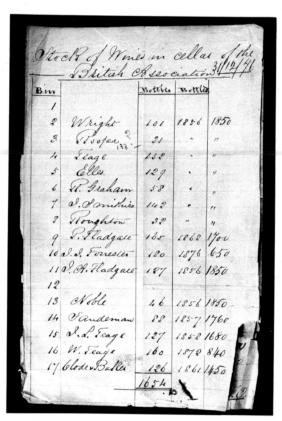

Extract from the Wine Stock List, 1876
(prices shown in last column)

The Factory House at Oporto

18

Forrester and the controversy ☆ When was Port fully fortified ☆ The Factory wines in the Douro District ☆ Evidence of W. H. G. Kingston

In assessing the high consumption of port at that time, two important considerations must be taken into account, namely to what extent port was then fully fortified and also the contents of the bottles.

James Forrester, in his evidence before the Select Committee of the House of Commons in 1852 on the subject of the duties on wines into the United Kingdom, stated that the proportion of brandy added 'depended entirely upon the character of the wine required by the shipper'. In reply to a further question he said 'there is no Portwine that comes to this country that has less brandy in it than about three gallons a pipe. The heavy brandied rich wine cannot ever contain less than 15/17 gallons per pipe'. The latter figure is an average equivalent of 72 litres per pipe, compared with the minimum of 105 litres added nowadays.

Forrester was an advocate of allowing 'the fermentation to take its natural course to produce a dry wine and a pure wine'. In that case any brandy that was added was solely to keep the wine sound. He did however agree that 'if a rich wine (i.e. Sweet) be really required, the fermentation is checked and brandy is added'. That admission in 1852 shows that he was fighting a losing battle in his campaign to keep port as a barely fortified wine, in effect a strong burgundy. But we are still in doubt as to whether the final alcoholic strength was by that date as high as it eventually became.

An earlier writer the Reverend Kinsey in his account in *Portugal Illustrated* of a visit to Oporto in 1827 stated that 'about 2 almudes (50 litres) of brandy have been thrown into the pipe, which is with few exceptions all that it takes to England'. But thirty years earlier in 1797, a letter from Offley Forrester in Oporto to their London office mentioned that 'wine has been bought up for the Navy from farmers warranted to have 14 canadas (about 32 litres) of Brandy in a pipe'. Admittedly it was apparent from other sources as well that at that period the poorest wines were disposed of to the British Navy.

In 1845, Forrester had been at the centre of a heated controversy with many of the farmers in the Alto Douro, owing to his strongly expressed criticisms of the wines produced there and of the methods of tasting and selection employed in determining the wines classified as first class. A committee of farmers, based at Covas do Douro but representing a very large number of others over a wide area, whose names were listed in the press, published a strong denial of Forrester's assertions which, they claimed, had been made known not only in Portugal but also abroad. They accused him of trying to discredit their wines on the grounds that they were not 'genuine' and that they were adulterated with elderberry, sugar, molasses, brandy and *geropiga*. A copy of the publication *Periódico dos Pobres* dated Porto 3rd February 1845, in the possession of the British Association, reports all the correspondence and

Baron James Forrester
(1809–61)

lists the farmers concerned. The latter wrote from Sabrosa to the 'President and Members of the Factory House in Oporto' to refute Forrester's statements. They maintained that the growers of fine wines, in the best districts of the Douro, never adulterated their wines and that they only added a small amount of brandy which 'as everyone knows preserves and perfects the wine'. They also said that as regards the addition of *geropiga* which they did not consider an adulteration, this was not for wines destined for the British market, but for North and South American and for consumption in Portugal.

This controversy is of interest in the context of determining to what extent port at that period was a fully fortified wine and the conclusion is reached, if we are to believe Forrester's evidence, that in 1845 the fine wines were still being almost fully fermented, with only a small quantity of brandy added at the vintage, or perhaps later prior to shipment.

However the evidence of W. H. G. Kingston, given later, refutes this argument completely.

Before we leave Forrester, some other of his reports are of interest. He had mentioned a special commission being appointed in 1852 to report on the wines of the Douro and explained that 'in the Douro district there is a territorial division called the Demarcated area of the Factory. This area in the Alto Douro denoted the vineyards that produced Factory wines, that is those set apart solely for shipment to Great Britain and which had been classified as being of the first quality'. So it is clear that although the Factory in Oporto had in the collective sense ceased to exist as far back as 1810, yet the term when applied to certain wines was still in use over 40 years later.

[96]

The Factory House at Oporto

Forrester also stated that in 1853 a vineyard worker earned about 7d. per day and that the annual expense of growing one pipe varied between 15s. and £3 according to the nature of the ground. He also calculated that it took 1,000 vines, with an area of about 3,000m², to produce a pipe.

Joseph James Forrester was the nephew of James Forrester who had come to Oporto in 1803 and who was one of the founder members, described as from the former Factory, of the British Association until his death in Oporto in 1840. His nephew was born in Hull in 1809 of a family of Scottish origin and came to join the firm of Offley Webber Forrester in 1831. He was destined to become one of the most distinguished and at times controversial members of the port wine trade. He rendered outstanding services to the wine trade in Portugal, including surveys of the port wine district of the Douro valley and in 1848 a map of the River Douro from the mouth below Oporto to the Spanish frontier, as well as a map of the wine district itself. He published studies on the diseases of the vine and numerous works on the wine trade in Portugal. In 1851 he was awarded the first prize of 50 guineas for an 'Essay on Portugal', which had been offered in London by Benjamin Oliveira, F.R.S.

Forrester was created Barão de Forrester by the Portuguese Government and received decorations and medals in many other countries, including France, Spain, Russia, Sardinia, Austria and Italy. He was a talented painter in water-colour and painted many well-known personalities in Portugal both connected with the wine trade and the Douro wine district as well as statesmen, naval and military men. His picture of the Rua dos Inglezes, showing the figures of most of the British merchants of the time, was drawn in 1834 and is a remarkable work. An engraving of this picture hangs in the Factory House.

The controversy that he created with regard to the style and alcoholic strength of port has been related.

It was an irony of fate that this eminent member of the port trade was destined in 1861 to be drowned when his boat capsized in the upper River Douro, the river he knew so well and which he had surveyed in such detail.

Forrester was never a member of the British Association, which perhaps is not surprising in view of his controversial views which did not endear him to the Factory. He was invited to dinners at the Factory House in 1833 and 1834, but there is no record as to whether he was ever proposed for membership.

However the question did not arise a few years later, as on 13th of November 1840 his firm, then called Offley & Webber, wrote to the British Association to inform them that in consequence of the death of their late Partner, Mr. James Forrester (that is the uncle of the Baron), and neither of their present Partners being members of the Association, their subscription would cease at the end of the present year. (They were not to re-join until 1876.)

W. H. G. Kingston was a member of the British Association in Oporto and a Partner in the firm Lambert Kingston & Egan. He wrote in *Lusitanian Sketches* (1845) that attempts had been made to have port wine without brandy. This was clearly a reference to Forrester's theories. He further stated that 'every respectable merchant in Oporto declares that it cannot be shipped to England without a certain quantity of brandy to preserve its quality and that those persons who pretend to do so most grievously deceive their correspondents'. Kingston also made it plain that the addition of brandy 'at the very critical moment, so difficult to decide, before that stage which produces the

Chapter 18

bitterness commences' was made in order to retain some of the sweetness and richness in the wine and to prevent it fermenting right out. It is unfortunate that he does not mention exactly how much was the 'certain quantity of brandy' that the respectable merchants added. At least it confirms that by that date (1845) there was no question of the brandy being added after fermentation merely to preserve the wine during shipment. That system must have ceased before then, but at the same time it is unlikely that port was fortified up to anything like the same alcoholic strength as we know it today much before the middle of the 19th century. The evidence available does not support those writers who have suggested that it was much earlier.

Kingston was the son of L. H. Kingston who had been elected a member of the Association in 1817. He became well-known later as a writer of children's books. In *Lusitanian Sketches* he gave advice to his readers on the subject of port, 'the shortest time Port wine, to give it fair play, ought to be kept in bottle, is two years; four improves it more and in six it reaches perfection'. He continues 'By age alone ought Port to be classed, of the different qualities, first stands the old tawny Port, grown old in cask . . . if your wine merchant assures you that it was shipped to him by one of the first Oporto houses and that he had had it bottled in his cellars five or six years, you may feel confident that you are drinking a very fine wine'.

If that represented the general view of those times, then it is certainly in disagreement with what is advocated nowadays, that tawny port shows at its best if drunk as soon as possible after being drawn from the cask, and that bottle-age does not improve it.

On vintage port, Kingston was less explicit, beyond saying that 'the wine most suited to the fogs and cold of the English autumn, winter and early spring is the rich, generous, rosy wine, such as that of the famed Vintage of 1834, and of the late ones of equal credit of 1840 and 1842'. Unfortunately he gave no indication as to the age at which it should be bottled.

Kingston was elected a member of the British Association in Oporto in 1841, but evidently lived mostly in London where he enjoyed the society life and achieved some literary distinction. He was most anxious to mix with what he considered to be the best Portuguese society, which he thought most of the British in Oporto were unable to do. His observations were at times condescending and he clearly considered that not all the Oporto families, whether Portuguese or British, were of the social standing of those with whom he was accustomed to mix in England. 'Many English residents not mixing in the more select circles have been unable to form a correct opinion on the subject: indeed I know of few writers on the country who have enjoyed opportunities of observing the higher classes correctly. In speaking of Oporto they (the British) must not be forgotten, for though forming but a small portion of society, they are tolerably conspicuous. There are about fifty families, a part only of whom move in the higher circles and are much respected by the Portuguese . . . they inhabit some of the best houses in the most airy parts of the city. There is no city in the Peninsular where an English family can enjoy so much comfort and independence'. However he could not very well criticise his fellow members of the Factory: 'I must pay a tribute which I consider due to the British merchants of Oporto. I believe that there is not to be found a more gentlemanly honourable set of men in any of the mercantile communities in other parts of the world than are the gentlemen of the British Factory: though a person who has written lately about the Port

The Factory House at Oporto

Wine Trade has, with most reckless disregard of truth, ventured to asperse their character'. A clear reference to Baron Forrester, who was always at loggerheads with the Factory.

Kingston also paid tribute 'to the name of my friend Mr. John Graham who from his liberal and amiable disposition and noble generosity on all occasions, is an honour to his profession'.

He also wrote at length about the vintage in the Douro wine region, where he claimed that about 30,000 workers were engaged, including women and children, and of these 20,000 were Gallegos from Galicia, who were employed in carrying the baskets of grapes from the vineyards to the treading tanks (*lagares*). The Spaniards returned home with twenty to thirty shillings, although some remained to work throughout the year. 'They as well as the Portuguese labourers receive from eightpence to fourteenpence a day, and women who perform the lighter work about fourpence, which enables them to live in tolerable comfort'.

He wrote interestingly about the journey from Oporto to the wine district. 'In the times when the Oporto merchants appeared on the Exchange in bag wigs and swords, the journey to Regoa was considered a most arduous undertaking, invariably occupying three days (albeit the road was in a far better state than at present) while each night was spent in feasting and good fellowship, some six or eight gentlemen always travelling together, with three or four attendants each. Even in later years they invariably proceeded in a dignified style, at the rate of fifteen to twenty miles a day. But now each merchant goes up by himself to make his purchases when he thinks fit and gets over the ground as fast as he can'. The route taken was through Penafiel, Vila Meão and Amarante to the summit of the Quintella pass, which Kingston reached on horseback in one day from Oporto. 'There is one of the best inns in Portugal. I have described so many bad inns in Portugal that it is but justice to say that this one has an entrance separate both from the stable and the kitchen, that all the apartments are on one floor with large sitting rooms and bedrooms adjoining. With these various recommendations it is a favourite resort of most travellers to the Douro. All the windows are glazed, a luxury to be found in few inns, though at the same time it is destitute of fire-places which are much required in this elevated and cold region'. In fact the inn at Quintella also described by Kingston as 'a hospitable mansion', was praised by other writers, but it is hard to identify any building still standing there now with that which the 19th century travellers considered so fine.

Kinsey had written in 1828 that the Estalagem at Quintella was 'reputed to be the best in Portugal, and as we found furnished with every comfort which the most fastidious traveller could desire. In addition to fine suites of apartments, a large public dining-room and bedchambers vying in comfort and cleanliness with those of any English hotel, we observed a large handsome bar in the house, after the fashion of our inns, from which every article required was delivered with the utmost promptitude'.

It seems rather exaggerated praise, but it perhaps was a comparative reflection on the very poor standard of accommodation available elsewhere in the countryside in Portugal at that time.

A final interesting note about the journey in the old days to the Douro vineyards comes from an official dispatch issued in Lisbon in 1753 which gave permission for British merchants of good fame and character to bear arms when going up-country to buy wines in remote and bandit-infested regions.

Chapter 18

19

Early sales in London ☆ First mentions of Vintage Port and individual shippers ☆ Size of old bottles

The description 'Port Wine' was in general use in England by the middle of the 18th century and the first mention of Port by Christie's in London was in their catalogue in 1768. However the shippers in Oporto continued to refer to red or white wines until later. Hunt Roope in 1759 invoiced red wine of the 1756 and 1757 vintages and a pipe of white wine, but by 1785 they were referring to Port Wine and in 1794 they recorded a pipe of Port wine for Lord Rodney and in 1796 'four pipes of best Red Port for reverend gentlemen at Eton College'. Croft's early records mention a shipment of Red Port wine in 1812, but Offley Forrester used the full description only several years later. In Ireland a 'new duty on Port Wines' was reported from Dublin in 1796.

Records survive of shipments from Oporto in 1701 by the firm of Stevenson & Allen, Merchants, in which red wine was sold at £27 per pipe and white at £23. If the size of the cask quoted was the same as now, then these prices appear extremely high considering that port was being shipped at prices even lower about two centuries later. Surprisingly the same firm exported *stum* (unfermented grape juice) at £14 per hogshead, that is slightly higher in price than the wine.

At the early sales in London, the ports were described as just Red or White Port, with the name of the U.K. wine merchant or private seller. The first sale of port at Christie's was in 1768, when the 'Port' sold for 15s. 6d. a dozen and the 'White Port' for 17s. 6d. This was described as 'a Sale for an Innkeeper and Farmer at the White Hart and Post Office, Petersfield'.

In 1773 came the first mention in a Christie catalogue of a vintage date, the 1765. The same year the sale of port in cask was first recorded: 13 pipes of 1767 were sold for £35 a pipe. This would appear to have been a very high price, but the size of the cask is in doubt, as well as the basis on which the price was calculated. By 1787 the content of a pipe was specified as 138 gallons, which would be nearer the size of a lodge or storage cask and definitely much larger than the normal present day shipping pipe. However, by 1801 the contents of a pipe had come down to 125 gallons, but the price at £57 19s. 5d. still appears very high. In 1827 a hogshead of 56 gallons was sold, the same size as used today.

It was not until 1810 that a shipper's name (Croft) appeared in a Christie sale catalogue; and a two-year bottling was first mentioned for the 1820 and 1824, sold in 1827. This was most unusual at that time and Christie's, writing of the 1858 Sandeman bottled in 1860, remarked that it was 'a rare two year bottling at this period, three year bottlings more normal'.

From later auction catalogues, we find Cockburn first mentioned in 1838, Taylor, Fonseca & Offley in 1845 and Warre & Graham in 1852.

There appears to have been no standard practice as to the age at which the wines were shipped from Oporto. In most cases they were probably very young and for examples Offley shipped the 1813 at £48 per pipe in 1814 and the 1812 at £52. Croft shipped the 1820 in November 1821 and in the same year the 1815 at £50 'for immediate bottling'. The customer instructed 'He would be obliged by our selecting if it is in our power genuine 1815's, to be particularly soft, silky, full of colour and flavour, with no more Brandy than is sufficient to preserve them'. This theme tended to recur for many years and is evidence that the customers did not want highly fortified wines, and this applied also to royalty. In April 1822 Croft shipped five pipes Vintage 1820 No. 3 to Chalie & Richards in London and the following instructions were received: 'These wines intended for H. B. Majesty George the 4th. They must be a very soft silky rich high flavoured wine, to be particularly careful that there is no predominance of Brandy, a strong coarse and harsh wine being particularly objectionable to the Royal palate. We are recommended to exert ourselves to the utmost to give satisfaction'.

The same theme persisted in 1830 when a customer of Croft required the wine 'to be high flavoured soft and silky, full and rich but not to be deficient in colour and by no means to possess any heat of Brandy as it will be required for immediate bottling and use'.

Prices tended to fluctuate considerably during that period. Immediately after the Peninsular War prices were very high and in 1812 Croft shipped their 'Best Old' between £63 and £70 per pipe. By 1820 the price had dropped to £32 and this was still maintained in 1828.

In the early part of the 19th century there is evidence that port was considered to have some similarity to Burgundy. In 1816* there was a reference to two pipes 'Very Superior Rorez (sic) Port, the Burgundy grape' and in 1829† the 1802 vintage was described as 'exceeding curious of the highest quality and flavour', and the same vintage as 'Curious Old Port of high Burgundy flavours'.

Evidently the customers wanted the port to be a type of high-strength burgundy, hence the sales description, and earlier in 1807 Hunt Roope replied rather scathingly to a customer on this subject. 'Respecting Burgundy grape we know of none grown in this country by that denomination and we conceive it merely a finesse of certain houses with a view to amusing their correspondents with novel names for their superior wines'.

The size of the bottle used in the early days may have been smaller than the present day bottle, and this could partly explain the apparently high consumption. There is no reference to the size of the actual bottles in Factory House records until 1878, when a purchase of port in quart bottles was made, but much earlier in 1836 decanters described as quart and pint were bought.

In sales records in London there is little mention of the size, but some 1795 port was sold in 1813 in magnums, and there is a reference in 1845 to pints.

From an examination of collections of old wine bottles in the possession of London wine merchants, the older bottles used for port, at least those of the 18th century, would appear to be made of very thick glass and the punts at the base of the bottles were very deep, considerably reducing the content. Others appear to be little larger than a present day half-bottle. Possibly the larger bottles of that period were described as magnums, although in fact they held little more than the present quart.

*From the Christie archives: 16th June 1879.
†Catalogue dated 13th August 1829.

Chapter 19

20

From the earliest days the port supplied to the Factory House was in the names of the individual members and not of the shippers and this custom survived until well into this century in the case of vintage ports. More recently the member firms have contributed a quantity of each vintage declared by them while members on election to the Association present 14 or 15 dozen (a quarter cask) of any vintage of their choice.

This quantity is traditional since 1856. At that date the stock of port in the Factory House cellars was recorded as 192 dozen and evidently this was considered too low for it was decided 'that the stock be replenished by every member resident contributing 14 dozen of bottled Port'. Up to that time the same distinction was not drawn between vintage and tawny ports as is done now. This was possibly because most, if not all, of the ports then were in a sense 'vintage', that is wines of a single year, although the length of time they had been bottled varied considerably.

The cellars were modified and improved in 1986 by the incorporation of the space previously occupied by a Ladies cloakroom, which was moved to the site of the old staircase cellar. As a result the three Vintage Port cellars now adjoin each other and considerably more space is available.

The system whereby the individual members contributed the port, apparently without charge, can be said to have changed in 1872, when stocks were again running low and it was resolved 'that one pipe of Port wine be purchased at the expense of the House, not exceeding in cost the sum of Three hundred and fifty mil reis, to be used for ordinary consumption'. It was agreed to request Mr. Fladgate to supply the pipe of Port 'which that gentleman kindly assented to do'. This would seem to have been the first occasion on which red port was purchased from one of the member firms (Taylor) although in fact in this instance it was not from the Treasurer's own firm. The actual price paid was the equivalent of about £78, which seems an extremely high price for those days, but possibly it included the bottling charges.

Soon after this, about 1875, it became the custom for the Treasurer to supply the Luncheon Tawny Port during his term of office, but not free of charge, as has frequently been stated.

The use of the House by members for private dinners was first authorised in 1841, with the proviso that a request should be made by four members and that it was allowed only on Thursdays. However, in 1876 the financial situation of the Association was evidently not satisfactory and in an attempt to increase the use of the House, a meeting on 10th January 1877 decided that Members, Honorary Members and Representatives were for the first time allowed to borrow the House for private dinners. For these occasions they could buy the Factory Luncheon Port at 2s. 6d. a bottle. An interesting comparison in prices shows that in London an 1870 port bottled in 1873 was sold in 1879 for 50s. a dozen while the earlier 1868 had been sold in 1878 for 42s.

Apparently table wines, including claret, were not charged for at lunch and it is hardly surprising that no profit was made, considering that in 1876 no less than 2,700 visitors 'attended the room for Luncheon'. As a result it was resolved that all wines, with the exception of Luncheon Port, be paid for separately. The prices fixed for the 'old clarets' such as a 'Lafitte 1864 and Léoville and Langoa of the same year' was 6s. 8d. per bottle, and for the younger claret, 'Old Bin' 1s. 9d. and 'New Bin' 1s. 6d. In fact the clarets were cheaper than the port. The prices were fixed by the House Committee 'to be regulated by their age in bottle'. A comparison with London prices shows that the same Lafitte '64 sold in London in 1889 for 11s. 6d. a bottle, a reasonable price considering the age of the wine at that date.

Champagne Lanson '74 was available at the Factory House for 9s. a bottle, and Ayala (second quality) at half the price. In London Pommery '74 was sold in 1889 for 17s. a bottle, a high price at the time.

Further interesting comparison can be found in a wine list, circa 1870, of the Oxford & Cambridge Club in London. The oldest port available was Christopher's 1820 at 21s. a bottle, seemingly a high price then, even for a fifty-year-old port. There were 15 other ports on the list, the cheapest being Christopher's 1858 at 4s. a bottle, 1s. a quarter bottle.

The only ports on the list described by the names of Oporto shippers were Kingston 1834 at 10s. 6d. and Holdsworth 'Old Gold'. In a later list, c. 1908, there were no fewer than 26 vintage ports, the oldest being Dow's 1863 at 14s. a bottle.

The members requiring 'Old Vintage Ports' were 'requested to order that such be decanted as nearly as possible six hours before they are required for consumption'.

In the same list were Château Léoville 1862 at 6s. and a Lafite at 7s., very similar in price to the 1864 at the Factory House. However the champagne was cheaper in London, with Bollinger, Heidsieck & Veuve Clicquot at 6s. 6d.

Until 1876 there was no mention in the accounts of any receipts for luncheons nor of the cost of the food provided. It would seem that the members paid direct to the *mordomo* (steward) who perhaps operated the dining room for his own account as one of his perks. However in that year the first mention of table money appears in the accounts, to a total of £85, against luncheon expenses of £92. The charge for lunch was the equivalent of 9d. and it was soon realised that this was too low and the price was increased so that in 1877 the account was balanced with receipts of £117 and expenses of £116.

An appropriate note on which to close is the sad reflection that the charge for lunch at the members' weekly lunch every Wednesday is now over sixty times higher than it was one hundred years ago.

Chapter 20

21 Conclusion

The main purpose of this work has been to record the origins and early history of the British Factories in the North of Portugal and to describe the building of the Factory House and its customs and contents.

From the middle of the 19th century and coinciding with the decline in British influence in Oporto, the records of the Association reveal little of historical interest and even in domestic matters they are remarkably lacking in details of any importance. This to some extent is an indication of the character of an institution where drastic innovation or change has never been favoured and where it is regarded as essential to preserve traditions in a world where such values are not nowadays always respected.

The members are aware of the need to safeguard the character of this historic and unique House, but to ensure this some degree of exclusiveness is unavoidable. Meanwhile, it continues to fulfil the role for which it was originally designed, as the social headquarters of the British Port shippers and as the scene of many functions and entertainments. An increasing number of visitors from all over the world invariably find the building of considerable historical interest and the contents and furnishings the more fascinating as they mostly date from the early 19th century and are preserved and in use in their original state and recorded in accounts from the makers and other documents on display in the recently formed Museum.

As the Factory House enters its third century, one is reminded of the words of Rose Macaulay (*They Went to Portugal*, Jonathan Cape, London, 1946), referring to the Oporto wine shippers:

'What a magnificent story for nearly three centuries is theirs, how picturesque their calling, how excitingly beautiful its setting, how rich their history in characters and incidents ... there is here a great romantic history.'

The Factory House is an important part of this history and the British Port shippers, conscious of the trust inherited from their predecessors, will most certainly not fail to maintain it in the future.

Bibliography

Manuscript Sources
British Association, Oporto: archives
British Library
Christie's, London: sales catalogues
Consul John Crispin: Report Relating to the Factory House at Oporto, 1830
Select Committee Report on Consular Establishments, 1812
Croft & Co., Vila Nova de Gaia: archives
Foreign Office, London: records
Gabinete de Historia da Cidade, Oporto: municipal archives
Guildhall Library, City of London: Foreign Register Section
Hunt, Roope & Co., Vila Nova de Gaia: archives
Offley, Forrester & Co., Vila Nova de Gaia: archives
Public Record Office, London: state papers
Taylor Fladgate & Yeatman, Vila Nova de Gaia: Joseph Camo letters

Published Sources
C. R. Boxer: 'The Portuguese Seaborne Empire 1415–1825', London, 1969
Sarah Bradford: 'The Story of Port', Christie's, 1978
Lord Carnavon: 'Portugal & Gallicia', London, 1836
Agostinho Rebello da Costa: 'Descripção Topográfica e Histórica da Cidade do Porto', 1789
Christie's, London: Annual Wine Review, 1972–1979
Arthur Costigan: 'Sketches of Society and Manners in Portugal', London 1787
John Croft: 'A Treatise on the Wines of Portugal', 1788
Richard Croker: 'Travels through Several Provinces of Spain and Portugal 1780–1781'
J. P. Cushion: 'Book of British Ceramic Marks', London
Major William Dalrymple: 'Travels through Spain and Portugal in 1774', 1777
John Delaforce: 'Anglicans Abroad, the History of the Chaplaincy and Church of St James Oporto', S.P.C.K., London, 1982
William Granville Eliot: 'A Treatise on the Defence of Portugal', 1811
J. A. Pinto Ferreira: 'A Praça da Ribeira', Oporto, 1953
Joseph James Forrester: 'Portugal and Its Capabilities', London, 1852
'A Gentleman Many Years Resident in Lisbon': 'A Picture of Lisbon', London, 1809
W. H. Harrison: 'The Tourist in Portugal', London, 1839
Lady Holland: Journal, 1808
James Jenifer: Journal of the 'Saudades', 1673

W. H. G. Kingston: 'Lusitanian Sketches', 1845

Reverend W. H. Kinsey: 'Portugal Illustrated', London, 1828

Pinho Leal: 'Portugal Antigo e Moderno', 1875, 1876, 1882

Carlos da Silva Lopes: 'Painting & Sculpture in Oporto during the 18th century', 1973

Rose Macaulay: 'They Went to Portugal', London, 1946

Marie-Thérèse Mandroux-França: Quantro Fases da Urbanização do Porto no Século XVIII, Boletim Cultural da Câmara Municipal do Porto, 2a Serie, Vol. 2, Oporto, 1984

John Milford jr: 'Peninsular Sketches', 1816

James Murphy: 'Travels in Portugal, 1789–1790', 1795

José Augusto França: 'A Arte em Portugal no Século XIX', 1966

Maria Helena Mendes Pinto: 'José Francisco de Paiva', Lisbon, 1973

P. W. Sandeman: 'The Story of Two Fine Wines', 1955

Charles Sellers: 'Oporto Old & New', London, 1899

Robert Southey: 'Letters from Spain & Portugal', 1797

H. Morse Stephens: 'Portugal', London, 1891

'The Story of Hunt Roope & Co, Oporto', London, 1953

René Taylor: 'The Architecture of Port Wine', Architectural Review, 1961

A. H. Walford: 'The British Factory in Lisbon', 1940

Walter Crum Watson: 'Portuguese Architecture', London, 1908

Thomas Woodmass: 'Letters to His Father', 1703/4

Philip Woodruff: 'The Men who Ruled India', 1953

R. B. and Mary Wragg: 'Carr in Portugal', Architectural Review, 1959

Appendix I: Member firms of the British Factory and British Association 1800–1990

This list of member firms of the British Factory and British Association 1800–1990, with dates of their election,* has been compiled from available records and is as complete as possible, but due to the frequent changes in the titles of the firms there may be errors or omissions. Dates prior to 1814 refer to members of the Factory before the foundation of the British Association in November that year, and the dates of their election are approximate. Firms marked ★ comprise the British Association in 1990.

1836	Allen Morgan & Co.		1802	Harris Brothers & Co.
1802	Babington Tidswell & Co.		1812	Harris & Co.
1802	Bearsley & Webb		1814	James Dawson Harris
1814	Burmester & Co.		1818	Harris, Quarles & Sons
1802	Burmester, Nash & Butler		1818	Harris, Quarles sen. J. D. Harris & Co.
1813	Butler & Co.		1825	Hely, P.
1814	Butler Tyndale & Co.		1827	Hely, P. & Co.
1819	Butler Naylor & Co.		1812	Hine, A. P.
1828	Butler Nephew & Co.		1876	Hooper Bros.
1816	Campbell Bowden & Taylor		1802	Hunt & Newman
1825	Campbell Taylor & Co.		1812	Hunt Newman & Roope
1802	Campion Offley Hesketh & Co.		1835	Hunt Roope Teage & Co.
1986	★ Churchill, Graham Lda		1907	Hunt Roope & Co.
1861	Clode & Baker		1850	Kingston & Sons
1816	Cockburn Wauchope & Co.		1813	Knowsley & Co.
1817	Cockburn Wauchope & Greig & Co.		1823	Knowsley & Nassau
1831	Cockburn Greig & Co.		1831	Knowsley, George
1835	Cockburn Greig & Dunlop		1802	Lambert Kingston & Co.
1848	★ Cockburn Smithes & Co.		1817	Lambert Kingston & Egan
1814	★ Croft & Co.		1850	Lambert & Co.
1800	Croft Thompson & Co.		1933	Mackenzie & Co.
1946	★ Delaforce Sons & Co.		1957	★ Martinez Gassiot & Co.
1814	Forster, John		1919	Morgan Bros.
1897	Gonzalez Byass & Co.		1882	Murat, H. T.
1818	Gould James Campbell & Co.		1811	Noble Perkins & Co.
1826	Gould & Co.		1825	Noble, J. H.
1835	Graham, John		1834	Noble, J. H. & Co.
1845	★ W. & J. Graham & Co.		1835	Noble, C. H. & Murat
1919	★ Guimaraens & Co.		1814	Offley Webber & Forrester

Editor's footnote: the author, after second thoughts, did not wish to include this list of member firms because it is possibly incomplete and not entirely correct. However, the list *is* of historical interest. Amendments or additions based on firm records will be welcomed by author and publisher.

1815	Offley Forrester & Co.	1860	Smith, T. I. Son & Johnston
1876	Offley Cramp & Forrester	1802	Snow, Thomas & Co.
1802	Page Noble & Co.	1814	Snow, William
1824	Page & Co.	1802	Stafford Swan·Knowsley & Co.
1834	Page, Chas.	1802	Stephenson Searle & Son
1845	Page, C. R. & Co.	1814	Swanns Knowsley & Co.
1802	Pennells Follett & Co.	1820	Swanns Knowsley & Nassau
1802	Perry Nassau & Thomsons	1814	Taylor & Co.
1834	Quillinan, J. T.	1826	Taylor, Joseph & Co.
1919	★ Robertson Bros. & Co.	1837	Taylor Fladgate & Co.
1860	Rocher Wigham & Co.	1844	★ Taylor Fladgate & Yeatman
1854	Roughton, William G.	1802	Thompson Croft & Co.
1814	Sandeman, George & Co.	1836	★ Warre & Co.
1849	★ Sandeman & Co.	1818	Waters T. M. & Co.
1856	Sandeman, Thomas G.	1813	Webb & Co.
1917	★ Silva & Cosens	1808	Webb Campbell Gray & Camo
1835	Smith, T. I.	1814	Webb Campbell Gray & Co.
1845	Smith Woodhouse & Co.	1876	Vanzeller & Co.

Appendix II: Individual Members of the British Association (Factory House) 1800–1990

This list of individual members of the British Association (Factory House) 1800–1990, with dates of their election, includes members resident in England and Scotland and some who lived temporarily in Portugal. Dates prior to 1812 are approximate and refer to members of the old Factory, full details of whom are not available due to lack of records. ★ Denotes present member.

1879		Adam, Charles R.	1815		Crispin, John
1918		Adam, James G.	1908		Croft, Francis E.
1835		Allen, John	1811		Croft, Frederick
1933		Andrews, W. E.	1875		Croft, Sir John, Bt.
1984	★	Bain, David G. S.	1964	★	Delaforce, David J.
1902		Baker, Charles	1946		Delaforce, Henry J.
1925		Baker, C. H.	1876		Delaforce, George H.
1926		Baker, Eric G. C.	1946	★	Delaforce, John de F.
1866		Baker, George jr.	1980		Delaforce, Richard A.
1902		Baker, George C.	1946		Delaforce, Victor S. de F.
1957		Barnett, C. P.	1835		Dunlop, Hugh
1962	★	Bower, Maurice H. S.	1960	★	Eastaugh, Gilbert E. M.
1973		Bull, Jeremy E.	1952		Edwards, Peter S.
1811		Burmester, Frederick	1830		Egan, Edward jr.
1980	★	Burnett, John K.	1882		Elles, G. B.
1839		Butler, Charles	1839		Elles, Malcolm J.
1802		Butler, James	1868		Fladgate, Francis P. G.
1917		Byass, R. C.	1838		Fladgate, John A.
1897		Byass, R. W.	1929		Flower, Harold M.
1834		Callanane, William	1933		Flower, Leonard R.
1811		Camo, Joseph	1875		Forrester, Frank W.
1878		Campbell, H. G. L.	1811		Forrester, James
1875		Clode, Nathaniel	1875		Forrester, Joseph James
1875		Cobb, Charles D.	1875		Forrester, William Offley
1899		Cobb, Edward W.	1818		Forster, Albert
1980	★	Cobb, Peter M.	1875		Forster, John C.
1919		Cobb, Reginald F.	1813		Foster, John
1928		Cobb, Reginald M.	1922		Gilbey, A. R.
1903		Cobb, William M.	1922		Gilbey, S. W.
1830		Cockburn, Alexander	1922		Gilbey, W. Gordon
1841		Cockburn, Archibald	1846		Godfrey, John Richard
1924		Cockburn, Ernest H.	1855		Godfrey, William
1929		Cockburn, Frederick A.	1922		Gold, A. H.
1899		Cockburn, Moncrieff	1891		Gonne, Arthur E.
1876		Crawford, William S.	1825		Gonne, Charles

1875	Gonne, Edward
1875	Gonne, William
1929	Gore-Langton, G. M.
1825	Gould, Gerard
1897	Graham, Donald
1959	Graham, G. C. B.
1909	Graham, G. M. A.
1897	Graham, James N.
1904	Graham, J. D.
1904	Graham, J. F.
1834	Graham, John
1986 ★	Graham, John L.
1930	Graham, J. Gerard
1937	Graham, J. St. John
1951	Graham, Kenneth M.
1851	Graham, Robert jr.
1933	Grant, G. A.
1815	Greig, William
1922	Grinling, Arthur G.
1962 ★	Guimaraens, Bruce D. F.
1953	Guimaraens, Charles B. F.
1919	Guimaraens, Frank F.
1919	Guimaraens, George P.
1975 ★	Guimaraens, J. Gordon
1930	Guimaraens, Patrick H.
1914	Hadrill, H. C.
1875	Hadrill, H. J.
1813	Harris, James D.
1802	Harris, Quarles
1812	Harris, William R.
1964	Hawkings-Byass, G. W.
1964	Hawkings-Byass, J. A.
1965 ★	Heath, Trevor T. S.
1984	Heath, Nicholas J.
1825	Hely, Patrick
1984 ★	Higgins, Thomas N.
1811	Hine, A. P.
1876	Hooper, J. K.
1876	Hooper, J. K. jr.
1821	Hunt, Arthur
1875	Hunt, Thomas N.
1871	Hutcheson, Stewart S.
1961 ★	Jennings, H. Gwyn
1919	Kendall, Albert C.
1817	Kingston, Lucy H.
1841	Kingston, William H.
1851	Kingston, Charles
1811	Knowsley, George
1845	Lambert, John
1854	Lambert, T.
1917	Lawson, Edward D.

1930	Leslie, Francis S.
1947	Mackenzie, Ian K.
1933	Mackenzie, Kenneth N.
1957	McLean, Donald H.
1898	Milne, J. G.
1919	Morgan, James E.
1887	Muir, M. E.
1875	Murat, Henry T.
1900	Murat, John, H. Q.
1832	Nassau, Henry
1819	Naylor, Daniel
1896	Newman, R. D.
1936	Newman, Sir R. D., Bt.
1892	Newman, R. L.
1811	Newman, Thomas H.
1836	Newman, Thomas
1875	Newman, Thomas N.
1831	Noble, Charles H.
1806	Noble, John H.
1851	Noble, John P.
1851	Noble, Richard H.
1929	Norris, O. T.
1929	Norris, W. S.
1975	Orr, David B.
1902	Page, Cecil G. L.
1824	Page, Charles
1842	Page, C. R.
1914	Pheysey, Herbert W.
1834	Quillinan, John T.
1988 ★	Reader, Hilary P.
1876	Reid, George
1963	Reid, Nevile
1962 ★	Reid, Robin A.
1969 ★	Robertson, Alastair B.
1963	Robertson, George F.
1919	Robertson-Rodger, J. N.
1811	Roope, Cabel (1)
1848	Roope, Cabel (2)
1878	Roope, Cabel (3)
1933	Roose, G. U. B.
1933	Roose, H. H.
1854	Roughton, William G.
1876	Sandeman, Albert G.
1954 ★	Sandeman, David P.
1876	Sandeman, Fleetwood G.
1815	Sandeman, George G.
1920	Sandeman, H. G. W.
1876	Sandeman, John G.
1952	Sandeman, Patrick W.
1952 ★	Sandeman, Timothy W.
1822	Sandeman, Thomas G.

1969	Sellers, Michael W.	1866	Teage, William R.
1841	Shorter, John	1841	Thomson, John R.
1975	Sinclair, Ian S.	1811	Tyndale, John
1887	Skeffington, Charles N.	1908	Urwick, Douglas R.
1957	Smith, Geoffrey B.	1957	Vigne, Felix St. B.
1860	Smith, G. W.	1917	Warre, Amyas F.
1834	Smith, T. I.	1928	Warre, Francis R.
1914	Smithes, Archibald C.	1836	Warre, George
1848	Smithes, Henry	1917	Warre, George F.
1941	Smithes, John H.	1800	Warre, James
1855	Smithes, John T.	1957	Warre, J. A.
1811	Snow, William	1924	Warre, Philip A.
1904	Stewart, Robert	1800	Warre, William
1975	★ Symington, Amyas J.	1958	Warre, William A.
1906	Symington, Andrew J.	1818	Waters, Thomas M.
1958	★ Symington, Ian D. F.	1811	Weaver, Samuel
1989	★ Symington, John A. D.	1859	Wigham, Thomas
1929	Symington, John D.	1949	Williams, Charles R.
1964	★ Symington, James R. O'C.	1934	Williams, C. D.
1955	★ Symington, Michael D.	1834	Woodhouse, Robert
1924	Symington, Maurice M.	1841	Wright, Joseph R.
1983	★ Symington, Paul D.	1891	Wright, Charles
1975	★ Symington, Peter R.	1891	Yates, James A.
1929	Symington, Ronald A.	1929	Yeatman, E. Stanley
1934	Taylor, F. H.	1899	Yeatman, Frank P. S.
1814	Taylor, Joseph	1885	Yeatman, Harry O.
1882	Teage, Dixon W.A.	1875	Yeatman, Morgan
1858	Teage, John L.	1951	Yeatman, Morgan C.
1893	Teage, John L. jr.	1926	Yeatman, Richard S.
1821	Teage, Nicholas D. L.		

Appendix III: British Consuls in Oporto

1642	Nicholas Comerforde	
1659	Walter Maynard	Vice-Consul
1678	Edward Murcot	Vice-Consul
1690–1716	John Lee	
1716	David Jackson	Wine Shipper
1745–1748	J. B. Parker	
1748–1756	Robert Jackson	Wine Shipper
1756–1802	John Whitehead	Elected by the Factory August 1756
1802–1807	William Warre	Nominated by the Factory December 1802
1813–1832	John Crispin	Previously Consul & member of Factory in Lisbon
1826	John Hatt Noble	Pro-Consul
1832–1834	Colonel Thomas Sorell	
1834–1857	Edwin J. Johnston	
1858–1866	R. L. Swift	
1866–1891	Oswald J. Crawfurd	
1890	Honorius Grant	Vice-Consul
1891–1897	F. H. Newton	
1897–1903	Commander Malcolm H. Drummond, R.N. Retd.	
1903–1921	Honorius Grant	
1921–1922	R. Bernal	
1923–1927	C. A. Edmond	
1927–1931	G. L. Rogers	
1929–1949	H. W. Coverley	Vice-Consul
1931–1933	H. W. W. Bird	
1934	Stanley H. Gudgeon	
1936	J. K. V. Dible	
1938	M. A. B. Denton-Thompson	
1941	H. W. Reid Brown	
1944	C. G. Kemball	
1947–1952	R. B. Tollinton, C.M.G.	Consul-General
1952–1955	Lt. Commander W. B. C. Weld-Forrester, R.N. Retd.	Consul-General
1955–1958	A. D. Francis, C.B.E., M.V.O.	Consul-General
1958–1961	A. J. S. Pullan	Consul-General
1962–1968	B. C. MacDermot, C.M.G.	Consul-General
1968–1970	T. C. Sharman, O.B.E.	Consul-General
1970–1975	S. Lockhart, C.M.G., O.B.E.	Honorary Consul
1975–1977	C.R. Wrigley, O.B.E.	Honorary Consul
1978–1980	O. E. Goddard, O.B.E.	Consul
1980–1983	I. R. Murray	Consul
1983–1987	D. G. Ward	Consul
1987–	P. H. Gay	

Index